THE FIRST PART
OF
KING HENRY
THE FOURTH

WILLIAM SHAKESPEARE

1st WORLD
LIBRARY
Literary Society

YA
SHAK

THE FIRST PART OF KING HENRY THE FOUTH
WILLIAM SHAKESPEARE

© 1st World Library - Literary Society, 2005
PO Box 2211
Fairfield, IA 52556
www.1stworldlibrary.org
First Edition

LCCN: 2005927845
Softcover ISBN: 1-4218-1346-7
Hardcover ISBN: 1-4218-1308-4
eBook ISBN: 1-4218-1384-X

Purchase *"The First Part of King Henry The Fourth"*
as a traditional bound book at:
www.1stWorldLibrary.org/purchase.asp?ISBN=1-4218-1346-7

1st World Library Literary Society is a nonprofit organization
dedicated to promoting literacy by:

Creating a free internet library accessible from any
computer worldwide.
Hosting writing competitions and offering book
publishing scholarships.

Readers interested in supporting literacy
through sponsorship, donations or
membership please contact:
literacy@1stworldlibrary.org
Check us out at: www.1stworldlibrary.org
and start downloading free ebooks today.

*The First Part of King Henry
The Fourth*
contributed by the Charles Family
in support of
1st World Library Literary Society

DRAMATIS PERSONAE

KING HENRY THE FOURTH
HENRY, Prince of Wales, son to the King
PRINCE JOHN OF LANCASTER, son to the King
EARL OF WESTMORELAND
SIR WALTER BLUNT
THOMAS PERCY, Earl of Worcester.
HENRY PERCY, Earl of Northumberland
HENRY PERCY, surnamed Hotspur, his son
EDMUND MORTIMER, Earl of March
RICHARD SCROOP, Archbishop of York
ARCHIBALD, Earl of Douglas
OWEN GLENDOWER
SIR RICHARD VERNON

SIR JOHN FALSTAFF
SIR MICHAEL, a friend to the Archbishop of York
POINS
GADSHILL
PETO
BARDOLPH
LADY PERCY, wife to Hotspur, and sister to Mortimer
LADY MORTIMER, daughter to Glendower, and wife to Mortimer
MISTRESS QUICKLY, hostess of the Boar's Head in Eastcheap
Lords, Officers, Sheriff, Vintner, Chamberlain, Drawers, two Carriers, Travellers, and Attendants

SCENE: *England and Wales*

ACT I

SCENE I

London. The Palace

Enter the KING, LORD JOHN OF LANCASTER,
EARL OF WESTMORELAND, SIR WALTER BLUNT,
with others

KING. So shaken as we are, so wan with care,
Find we a time for frighted peace to pant
And breathe short-winded accents of new broils
To be commenc'd in stronds afar remote.

No more the thirsty entrance of this soil
Shall daub her lips with her own children's blood.
No more shall trenching war channel her fields,
Nor Bruise her flow'rets with the armed hoofs
Of hostile paces. Those opposed eyes
Which, like the meteors of a troubled heaven,
All of one nature, of one substance bred,
Did lately meet in the intestine shock
And furious close of civil butchery,
Shall now in mutual well-beseeming ranks
March all one way and be no more oppos'd
Against acquaintance, kindred, and allies.
The edge of war, like an ill-sheathed knife,
No more shall cut his master. Therefore, friends,
As far as to the sepulchre of Christ-
Whose soldier now, under whose blessed cross
We are impressed and engag'd to fight-
Forthwith a power of English shall we levy,
Whose arms were moulded in their mother's womb
To chase these pagans in those holy fields
Over whose acres walk'd those blessed feet
Which fourteen hundred years ago were nail'd
For our advantage on the bitter cross.
But this our purpose now is twelvemonth old,
And bootless 'tis to tell you we will go.
Therefore we meet not now. Then let me hear
Of you, my gentle cousin Westmoreland,
What yesternight our Council did decree
In forwarding this dear expedience.

EARL OF WESTMORELAND. My liege, this haste
was hot in question
And many limits of the charge set down
But yesternight; when all athwart there came
A post from Wales, loaden with heavy news;
Whose worst was that the noble Mortimer,
Leading the men of Herefordshire to fight
Against the irregular and wild Glendower,

Was by the rude hands of that Welshman taken,
A thousand of his people butchered;
Upon whose dead corpse there was such misuse,
Such beastly shameless transformation,
By those Welshwomen done as may not be
Without much shame retold or spoken of.

KING. It seems then that the tidings of this broil
Brake off our business for the Holy Land.

EARL OF WESTMORELAND. This, match'd with
other, did, my gracious lord;
For more uneven and unwelcome news
Came from the North, and thus it did import:
On Holy-rood Day the gallant Hotspur there,
Young Harry Percy, and brave Archibald,
That ever-valiant and approved Scot,
At Holmedon met,
Where they did spend a sad and bloody hour;
As by discharge of their artillery
And shape of likelihood the news was told;
For he that brought them, in the very heat
And pride of their contention did take horse,
Uncertain of the issue any way.

KING. Here is a dear, a true-industrious friend,
Sir Walter Blunt, new lighted from his horse,
Stain'd with the variation of each soil
Betwixt that Holmedon and this seat of ours,
And he hath brought us smooth and welcome news.
The Earl of Douglas is discomfited;
Ten thousand bold Scots, two-and-twenty knights,
Balk'd in their own blood did Sir Walter see
On Holmedon's plains. Of prisoners, Hotspur took
Mordake Earl of Fife and eldest son
To beaten Douglas, and the Earl of Athol,
Of Murray, Angus, and Menteith.
And is not this an honourable spoil?
A gallant prize? Ha, cousin, is it not?

EARL OF WESTMORELAND. In faith,
It is a conquest for a prince to boast of.

KING. Yea, there thou mak'st me sad, and mak'st me sin
In envy that my Lord Northumberland
Should be the father to so blest a son-
A son who is the theme of honour's tongue,
Amongst a grove the very straightest plant;
Who is sweet Fortune's minion and her pride;
Whilst I, by looking on the praise of him,
See riot and dishonour stain the brow
Of my young Harry. O that it could be prov'd
That some night-tripping fairy had exchang'd
In cradle clothes our children where they lay,
And call'd mine Percy, his Plantagenet!
Then would I have his Harry, and he mine.
But let him from my thoughts. What think you, coz,
Of this young Percy's pride? The prisoners
Which he in this adventure hath surpris'd
To his own use he keeps, and sends me word
I shall have none but Mordake Earl of Fife.

EARL OF WESTMORELAND. This is his uncle's teaching, this Worcester,
Malevolent to you In all aspects,
Which makes him prune himself and bristle up
The crest of youth against your dignity.

KING. But I have sent for him to answer this;
And for this cause awhile we must neglect
Our holy purpose to Jerusalem.
Cousin, on Wednesday next our council we
Will hold at Windsor. So inform the lords;
But come yourself with speed to us again;
For more is to be said and to be done
Than out of anger can be uttered.

EARL OF WESTMORELAND. I will my liege.

Exeunt

William Shakespeare

SCENE II

London. An apartment of the Prince's

Enter PRINCE OF WALES and SIR JOHN FALSTAFF

FALSTAFF. Now, Hal, what time of day is it, lad?

PRINCE. Thou art so fat-witted with drinking of old sack, and unbuttoning thee after supper, and sleeping upon benches after noon, that thou hast forgotten to demand that truly which thou wouldest truly know. What a devil hast thou to do with the time of the day, Unless hours were cups of sack, and minutes capons, and clocks the tongues of bawds, and dials the signs of leaping houses, and the blessed sun himself a fair hot wench in flame-coloured taffeta, I see no reason why thou shouldst be so superfluous to demand the time of the day.

FALSTAFF. Indeed you come near me now, Hal; for we that take purses go by the moon And the seven stars, and not by Phoebus, he, that wand'ring knight so fair. And I prithee, sweet wag, when thou art king, as, God save thy Grace-Majesty I should say, for grace thou wilt have none-

PRINCE. What, none?

FALSTAFF. No, by my troth; not so much as will serve to be prologue to an egg and butter.

PRINCE. Well, how then? Come, roundly, roundly.

FALSTAFF. Marry, then, sweet wag, when thou art king, let not us that are squires of the night's body be called thieves of the day's beauty. Let us be Diana's Foresters, Gentlemen of the Shade, Minions of the Moon; and let men say we be men of good government, being governed as the sea is, by our noble and chaste mistress the moon, under whose countenance we steal.

PRINCE. Thou sayest well, and it holds well too; for the

fortune of us that are the moon's men doth ebb and flow like the sea, being governed, as the sea is, by the moon. As, for proof now: a purse of gold most resolutely snatch'd on Monday night and most dissolutely spent on Tuesday morning; got with swearing 'Lay by,' and spent with crying 'Bring in'; now ill as low an ebb as the foot of the ladder, and by-and-by in as high a flow as the ridge of the gallows.

FALSTAFF. By the Lord, thou say'st true, lad- and is not my hostess of the tavern a most sweet wench?

PRINCE. As the honey of Hybla, my old lad of the castle- and is not a buff jerkin a most sweet robe of durance?

FALSTAFF. How now, how now, mad wag? What, in thy quips and thy quiddities? What a plague have I to do with a buff jerkin?

PRINCE. Why, what a pox have I to do with my hostess of the tavern?

FALSTAFF. Well, thou hast call'd her to a reckoning many a time and oft.

PRINCE. Did I ever call for thee to pay thy part?

FALSTAFF. No; I'll give thee thy due, thou hast paid all there.

PRINCE. Yea, and elsewhere, so far as my coin would stretch; and where it would not, I have used my credit.

FALSTAFF. Yea, and so us'd it that, were it not here apparent that thou art heir apparent- But I prithee, sweet wag, shall there be gallows standing in England when thou art king? and resolution thus fubb'd as it is with the rusty curb of old father antic the law? Do not thou, when thou art king, hang a thief.

PRINCE. No; thou shalt.

FALSTAFF. Shall I? O rare! By the Lord, I'll be a brave judge.

William Shakespeare

PRINCE. Thou judgest false already. I mean, thou shalt have the hanging of the thieves and so become a rare hangman.

FALSTAFF. Well, Hal, well; and in some sort it jumps with my humour as well as waiting in the court, I can tell you.

PRINCE. For obtaining of suits?

FALSTAFF. Yea, for obtaining of suits, whereof the hangman hath no lean wardrobe. 'Sblood, I am as melancholy as a gib-cat or a lugg'd bear.

PRINCE. Or an old lion, or a lover's lute.

FALSTAFF. Yea, or the drone of a Lincolnshire bagpipe.

PRINCE. What sayest thou to a hare, or the melancholy of Moor Ditch?

FALSTAFF. Thou hast the most unsavoury similes, and art indeed the most comparative, rascalliest, sweet young prince. But, Hal, I prithee trouble me no more with vanity. I would to God thou and I knew where a commodity of good names were to be bought. An old lord of the Council rated me the other day in the street about you, sir, but I mark'd him not; and yet he talked very wisely, but I regarded him not; and yet he talk'd wisely, and in the street too.

PRINCE. Thou didst well; for wisdom cries out in the streets, and no man regards it.

FALSTAFF. O, thou hast damnable iteration, and art indeed able to corrupt a saint. Thou hast done much harm upon me, Hal- God forgive thee for it! Before I knew thee, Hal, I knew nothing; and now am I, if a man should speak truly, little better than one of the wicked. I must give over this life, and I will give it over! By the Lord, an I do not, I am a villain! I'll be damn'd for never a king's son in Christendom.

PRINCE. Where shall we take a purse tomorrow, Jack?

FALSTAFF. Zounds, where thou wilt, lad! I'll make one. An I do not, call me villain and baffle me.

PRINCE. I see a good amendment of life in thee- from praying to purse-taking.

FALSTAFF. Why, Hal, 'tis my vocation, Hal. 'Tis no sin for a man to labour in his vocation.

Enter POINS

Poins! Now shall we know if Gadshill have set a match. O, if men were to be saved by merit, what hole in hell were hot enough for him? This is the most omnipotent villain that ever cried 'Stand!' to a true man.

PRINCE. Good morrow, Ned.

POINS. Good morrow, sweet Hal. What says Monsieur Remorse? What says Sir John Sack and Sugar? Jack, how agrees the devil and thee about thy soul, that thou soldest him on Good Friday last for a cup of Madeira and a cold capon's leg?

PRINCE. Sir John stands to his word, the devil shall have his bargain; for he was never yet a breaker of proverbs. He will give the devil his due.

POINS. Then art thou damn'd for keeping thy word with the devil.

PRINCE. Else he had been damn'd for cozening the devil.

POINS. But, my lads, my lads, to-morrow morning, by four o'clock early, at Gadshill! There are pilgrims gong to Canterbury with rich offerings, and traders riding to London with fat purses. I have vizards for you all; you have horses for yourselves.Gadshill lies to-night in Rochester. I have bespoke supper to-morrow night in Eastcheap. We may do it as secure as sleep. If you will go,

I will stuff your purses full of crowns; if you will not, tarry at home and be hang'd!

FALSTAFF. Hear ye, Yedward: if I tarry at home and go not, I'll hang you for going.

POINS. You will, chops?

FALSTAFF. Hal, wilt thou make one?

PRINCE. Who, I rob? I a thief? Not I, by my faith.

FALSTAFF. There's neither honesty, manhood, nor good fellowship in thee, nor thou cam'st not of the blood royal if thou darest not stand for ten shillings.

PRINCE. Well then, once in my days I'll be a madcap.

FALSTAFF. Why, that's well said.

PRINCE. Well, come what will, I'll tarry at home.

FALSTAFF. By the Lord, I'll be a traitor then, when thou art king.

PRINCE. I care not.

POINS. Sir John, I prithee, leave the Prince and me alone. I will lay him down such reasons for this adventure that he shall go.

FALSTAFF. Well, God give thee the spirit of persuasion and him the ears of profiting, that what thou speakest may move and what he hears may be believed, that the true prince may (for recreation sake) prove a false thief; for the poor abuses of the time want countenance. Farewell; you shall find me in Eastcheap.

PRINCE. Farewell, thou latter spring! farewell, All-hallown summer! *Exit FALSTAFF*

POINS. Now, my good sweet honey lord, ride with us tomorrow. I have a jest to execute that I cannot manage alone. Falstaff, Bardolph, Peto, and Gadshill shall rob those men that we have already waylaid; yourself and I will not be there; and when they have the booty, if you and I do not rob them, cut this head off from my shoulders.

PRINCE. How shall we part with them in setting forth?

POINS. Why, we will set forth before or after them and appoint them a place of meeting, wherein it is at our pleasure to fail; and then will they adventure upon the exploit themselves; which they shall have no sooner achieved, but we'll set upon them.

PRINCE. Yea, but 'tis like that they will know us by our horses, by our habits, and by every other appointment, to be ourselves.

POINS. Tut! our horses they shall not see- I'll tie them in the wood; our wizards we will change after we leave them; and, sirrah, I have cases of buckram for the nonce, to immask our noted outward garments.

PRINCE. Yea, but I doubt they will be too hard for us.

POINS. Well, for two of them, I know them to be as true-bred cowards as ever turn'd back; and for the third, if he fight longer than he sees reason, I'll forswear arms. The virtue of this jest will lie the incomprehensible lies that this same fat rogue will tell us when we meet at supper: how thirty, at least, he fought with; what wards, what blows, what extremities he endured; and in the reproof of this lies the jest.

PRINCE. Well, I'll go with thee. Provide us all things necessary and meet me to-night in Eastcheap. There I'll sup. Farewell.

POINS. Farewell, my lord.   *Exit*

PRINCE. I know you all, and will awhile uphold
The unyok'd humour of your idleness.
Yet herein will I imitate the sun,
Who doth permit the base contagious clouds
To smother up his beauty from the world,

That, when he please again to lie himself,
Being wanted, he may be more wond'red at
By breaking through the foul and ugly mists
Of vapours that did seem to strangle him.
If all the year were playing holidays,
To sport would be as tedious as to work;
But when they seldom come, they wish'd-for come,
And nothing pleaseth but rare accidents.
So, when this loose behaviour I throw off
And pay the debt I never promised,
By how much better than my word I am,
By so much shall I falsify men's hopes;
And, like bright metal on a sullen ground,
My reformation, glitt'ring o'er my fault,
Shall show more goodly and attract more eyes
Than that which hath no foil to set it off.
I'll so offend to make offence a skill,
Redeeming time when men think least I will.   *Exit*

SCENE III

London. The Palace

Enter the KING, NORTHUMBERLAND,
WORCESTER, HOTSPUR, SIR WALTER BLUNT,
with others

KING. My blood hath been too cold and temperate,
Unapt to stir at these indignities,
And you have found me, for accordingly
You tread upon my patience; but be sure
I will from henceforth rather be myself,
Mighty and to be fear'd, than my condition,
Which hath been smooth as oil, soft as young down,
And therefore lost that title of respect
Which the proud soul ne'er pays but to the proud.

WORCESTER. Our house, my sovereign liege, little
deserves
The scourge of greatness to be us'd on it-
And that same greatness too which our own hands
Have holp to make so portly.

NORTHUMBERLAND. My lord-

KING. Worcester, get thee gone; for I do see
Danger and disobedience in thine eye.
O, sir, your presence is too bold and peremptory,
And majesty might never yet endure
The moody frontier of a servant brow.
Tou have good leave to leave us. When we need
'Your use and counsel, we shall send for you.

                                    Exit WORCESTER

You were about to speak.

NORTHUMBERLAND. Yea, my good lord.
Those prisoners in your Highness' name demanded
Which Harry Percy here at Holmedon took,
Were, as he says, not with such strength denied
As is delivered to your Majesty.
Either envy, therefore, or misprision
Is guilty of this fault, and not my son.

HOTSPUR. My liege, I did deny no prisoners.
But I remember, when the fight was done,
When I was dry with rage and extreme toll,
Breathless and faint, leaning upon my sword,
Came there a certain lord, neat and trimly dress'd,
Fresh as a bridegroom; and his chin new reap'd
Show'd like a stubble land at harvest home.
He was perfumed like a milliner,
And 'twixt his finger and his thumb he held
A pouncet box, which ever and anon
He gave his nose, and took't away again;
Who therewith angry, when it next came there,
Took it in snuff; and still he smil'd and talk'd;

And as the soldiers bore dead bodies by,
He call'd them untaught knaves, unmannerly,
To bring a slovenly unhandsome corse
Betwixt the wind and his nobility.
With many holiday and lady terms
He questioned me, amongst the rest demanded
My prisoners in your Majesty's behalf.
I then, all smarting with my wounds being cold,
To be so pest'red with a popingay,
Out of my grief and my impatience
Answer'd neglectingly, I know not what-
He should, or he should not; for he made me mad
To see him shine so brisk, and smell so sweet,
And talk so like a waiting gentlewoman
Of guns and drums and wounds- God save the mark!-
And telling me the sovereignest thing on earth
Was parmacity for an inward bruise;
And that it was great pity, so it was,
This villanous saltpetre should be digg'd
Out of the bowels of the harmless earth,
Which many a good tall fellow had destroy'd
So cowardly; and but for these vile 'guns,
He would himself have been a soldier.
This bald unjointed chat of his, my lord,
I answered indirectly, as I said,
And I beseech you, let not his report
Come current for an accusation
Betwixt my love and your high majesty.

BLUNT. The circumstance considered, good my lord,
Whate'er Lord Harry Percy then had said
To such a person, and in such a place,
At such a time, with all the rest retold,
May reasonably die, and never rise
To do him wrong, or any way impeach
What then he said, so he unsay it now.

KING. Why, yet he doth deny his prisoners,
But with proviso and exception,

That we at our own charge shall ransom straight
His brother-in-law, the foolish Mortimer;
Who, on my soul, hath wilfully betray'd
The lives of those that he did lead to fight
Against that great magician, damn'd Glendower,
Whose daughter, as we hear, the Earl of March
Hath lately married. Shall our coffers, then,
Be emptied to redeem a traitor home?
Shall we buy treason? and indent with fears
When they have lost and forfeited themselves?
No, on the barren mountains let him starve!
For I shall never hold that man my friend
Whose tongue shall ask me for one penny cost
To ransom home revolted Mortimer.

HOTSPUR. Revolted Mortimer?
He never did fall off, my sovereign liege,
But by the chance of war. To prove that true
Needs no more but one tongue for all those wounds,
Those mouthed wounds, which valiantly he took
When on the gentle Severn's sedgy bank,
In single opposition hand to hand,
He did confound the best part of an hour
In changing hardiment with great Glendower.
Three times they breath'd, and three times did they
drink,
Upon agreement, of swift Severn's flood;
Who then, affrighted with their bloody looks,
Ran fearfully among the trembling reeds
And hid his crisp head in the hollow bank,
Bloodstained with these valiant cohabitants.
Never did base and rotten policy
Colour her working with such deadly wounds;
Nor never could the noble Mortimer
Receive so many, and all willingly.
Then let not him be slandered with revolt.

KING. Thou dost belie him, Percy, thou dost belie him!
He never did encounter with Glendower.

William Shakespeare

I tell thee
He durst as well have met the devil alone
As Owen Glendower for an enemy.
Art thou not sham'd? But, sirrah, henceforth
Let me not hear you speak of Mortimer.
Send me your prisoners with the speediest means,
Or you shall hear in such a kind from me
As will displease you. My Lord Northumberland,
We license your departure with your son.-
Send us your prisoners, or you will hear of it.

Exeunt KING, BLUNT, and Train

HOTSPUR. An if the devil come and roar for them,
I will not send them. I will after straight
And tell him so; for I will else my heart,
Albeit I make a hazard of my head.

NORTHUMBERLAND. What, drunk with choler?
Stay, and pause awhile.
Here comes your uncle.

Enter WORCESTER

HOTSPUR. Speak of Mortimer?
Zounds, I will speak of him, and let my soul
Want mercy if I do not join with him!
Yea, on his part I'll empty all these veins,
And shed my dear blood drop by drop in the dust,
But I will lift the downtrod Mortimer
As high in the air as this unthankful king,
As this ingrate and cank'red Bolingbroke.

NORTHUMBERLAND. Brother, the King hath made
your nephew mad.

WORCESTER. Who struck this heat up after I was
gone?

HOTSPUR. He will (forsooth) have all my prisoners;
And when I urg'd the ransom once again

Of my wive's brother, then his cheek look'd pale,
And on my face he turn'd an eye of death,
Trembling even at the name of Mortimer.

WORCESTER. I cannot blame him. Was not he proclaim'd
By Richard that dead is, the next of blood?

NORTHUMBERLAND. He was; I heard the proclamation.
And then it was when the unhappy King
(Whose wrongs in us God pardon!) did set forth
Upon his Irish expedition;
From whence he intercepted did return
To be depos'd, and shortly murdered.

WORCESTER. And for whose death we in the world's wide mouth
Live scandaliz'd and foully spoken of.

HOTSPUR. But soft, I pray you. Did King Richard then
Proclaim my brother Edmund Mortimer
Heir to the crown?

NORTHUMBERLAND. He did; myself did hear it.

HOTSPUR. Nay, then I cannot blame his cousin king,
That wish'd him on the barren mountains starve.
But shall it be that you, that set the crown
Upon the head of this forgetful man,
And for his sake wear the detested blot
Of murtherous subornation- shall it be
That you a world of curses undergo,
Being the agents or base second means,
The cords, the ladder, or the hangman rather?
O, pardon me that I descend so low
To show the line and the predicament
Wherein you range under this subtile king!
Shall it for shame be spoken in these days,
Or fill up chronicles in time to come,

That men of your nobility and power
Did gage them both in an unjust behalf
(As both of you, God pardon it! have done)
To put down Richard, that sweet lovely rose,
And plant this thorn, this canker, Bolingbroke?
And shall it in more shame be further spoken
That you are fool'd, discarded, and shook off
By him for whom these shames ye underwent?
No! yet time serves wherein you may redeem
Your banish'd honours and restore yourselves
Into the good thoughts of the world again;
Revenge the jeering and disdain'd contempt
Of this proud king, who studies day and night
To answer all the debt he owes to you
Even with the bloody payment of your deaths.
Therefore I say-

WORCESTER. Peace, cousin, say no more;
And now, I will unclasp a secret book,
And to your quick-conceiving discontents
I'll read you matter deep and dangerous,
As full of peril and adventurous spirit
As to o'erwalk a current roaring loud
On the unsteadfast footing of a spear.

HOTSPUR. If he fall in, good night, or sink or swim!
Send danger from the east unto the west,
So honour cross it from the north to south,
And let them grapple. O, the blood more stirs
To rouse a lion than to start a hare!

NORTHUMBERLAND. Imagination of some great
exploit
Drives him beyond the bounds of patience.

HOTSPUR. By heaven, methinks it were an easy leap
To pluck bright honour from the pale-fac'd moon,
Or dive into the bottom of the deep,
Where fadom line could never touch the ground,
And pluck up drowned honour by the locks,

So he that doth redeem her thence might wear
Without corrival all her dignities;
But out upon this half-fac'd fellowship!

WORCESTER. He apprehends a world of figures here,
But not the form of what he should attend.
Good cousin, give me audience for a while.

HOTSPUR. I cry you mercy.

WORCESTER. Those same noble Scots
That are your prisoners-

HOTSPUR. I'll keep them all.
By God, he shall not have a Scot of them!
No, if a Scot would save his soul, he shall not.
I'll keep them, by this hand!

WORCESTER. You start away.
And lend no ear unto my purposes.
Those prisoners you shall keep.

HOTSPUR. Nay, I will! That is flat!
He said he would not ransom Mortimer,
Forbade my tongue to speak of Mortimer,
But I will find him when he lies asleep,
And in his ear I'll holloa 'Mortimer.'
Nay;
I'll have a starling shall be taught to speak
Nothing but 'Mortimer,' and give it him
To keep his anger still in motion.

WORCESTER. Hear you, cousin, a word.

HOTSPUR. All studies here I solemnly defy
Save how to gall and pinch this Bolingbroke;
And that same sword-and-buckler Prince of Wales-
But that I think his father loves him not
And would be glad he met with some mischance,
I would have him poisoned with a pot of ale.

WORCESTER. Farewell, kinsman. I will talk to you
When you are better temper'd to attend.

NORTHUMBERLAND. Why, what a wasp-stung and
impatient fool
Art thou to break into this woman's mood,
Tying thine ear to no tongue but thine own!

HOTSPUR. Why, look you, I am whipp'd and scourg'd
with rods,
Nettled, and stung with pismires when I hear
Of this vile politician, Bolingbroke.
In Richard's time- what do you call the place-
A plague upon it! it is in Gloucestershire-
'Twas where the madcap Duke his uncle kept-
His uncle York- where I first bow'd my knee
Unto this king of smiles, this Bolingbroke-
'S blood!
When you and he came back from Ravenspurgh-

NORTHUMBERLAND. At Berkeley Castle.

HOTSPUR. You say true.
Why, what a candy deal of courtesy
This fawning greyhound then did proffer me!
Look, 'when his infant fortune came to age,'
And 'gentle Harry Percy,' and 'kind cousin'-
O, the devil take such cozeners!- God forgive me!
Good uncle, tell your tale, for I have done.

WORCESTER. Nay, if you have not, to it again.
We will stay your leisure.

HOTSPUR. I have done, i' faith.

WORCESTER. Then once more to your Scottish pris-
oners.
Deliver them up without their ransom straight,
And make the Douglas' son your only mean
For powers In Scotland; which, for divers reasons
Which I shall send you written, be assur'd
Will easily be granted. [To NORTHUMBERLAND]
You, my lord,
Your son in Scotland being thus employ'd,

Shall secretly into the bosom creep
Of that same noble prelate well-belov'd,
The Archbishop.

HOTSPUR. Of York, is it not?

WORCESTER. True; who bears hard
His brother's death at Bristow, the Lord Scroop.
I speak not this in estimation,
As what I think might be, but what I know
Is ruminated, plotted, and set down,
And only stays but to behold the face
Of that occasion that shall bring it on.

HOTSPUR. I smell it. Upon my life, it will do well.

NORTHUMBERLAND. Before the game is afoot thou
still let'st slip.

HOTSPUR. Why, it cannot choose but be a noble plot.
And then the power of Scotland and of York
To join with Mortimer, ha?

WORCESTER. And so they shall.

HOTSPUR. In faith, it is exceedingly well aim'd.

WORCESTER. And 'tis no little reason bids us speed,
To save our heads by raising of a head;
For, bear ourselves as even as we can,
The King will always think him in our debt,
And think we think ourselves unsatisfied,
Till he hath found a time to pay us home.
And see already how he doth begin
To make us strangers to his looks of love.

HOTSPUR. He does, he does! We'll be reveng'd on him.

WORCESTER. Cousin, farewell. No further go in this
Than I by letters shall direct your course.
When time is ripe, which will be suddenly,
I'll steal to Glendower and Lord Mortimer,
Where you and Douglas, and our pow'rs at once,

As I will fashion it, shall happily meet,
To bear our fortunes in our own strong arms,
Which now we hold at much uncertainty.

NORTHUMBERLAND. Farewell, good brother. We
shall thrive, I trust.

HOTSPUR. Uncle, adieu. O, let the hours be short
Till fields and blows and groans applaud our sport!

Exeunt

ACT II

SCENE I

Rochester. An inn yard

Enter a CARRIER with a lantern in his hand

1. CARRIER. Heigh-ho! an it be not four by the day, I'll be hang'd. Charles' wain is over the new chimney, and yet our horse not pack'd.- What, ostler!

OST. *[Within]* Anon, anon.

1. CARRIER. I prithee, Tom, beat Cut's saddle, put a few flocks in the point. Poor jade is wrung in the withers out of all cess.

Enter another CARRIER

2. CARRIER. Peas and beans are as dank here as a dog, and that is the next way to give poor jades the bots. This house is turned upside down since Robin Ostler died.

1. CARRIER. Poor fellow never joyed since the price of oats rose. It was the death of him.

2. CARRIER. I think this be the most villanous house in all London road for fleas. I am stung like a tench.

1. CARRIER. Like a tench I By the mass, there is ne'er a king christen could be better bit than I have been since the first cock.

2. CARRIER. Why, they will allow us ne'er a jordan, and then we leak in your chimney, and your chamber-lye breeds fleas like a loach.

1. CARRIER. What, ostler! come away and be hang'd! come away!

2. CARRIER. I have a gammon of bacon and two razes of ginger, to be delivered as far as Charing Cross.

1. CARRIER. God's body! the turkeys in my pannier are quite starved. What, ostler! A plague on thee! hast thou never an eye in thy head? Canst not hear? An 'twere not as good deed as drink to break the pate on thee, I am a very villain. Come, and be hang'd! Hast no faith in thee?

Enter GADSHILL

GADSHILL. Good morrow, carriers. What's o'clock?

1. CARRIER. I think it be two o'clock.

GADSHILL. I prithee lend me this lantern to see my gelding in the stable.

1. CARRIER. Nay, by God, soft! I know a trick worth two of that, i' faith.

GADSHILL. I pray thee lend me thine.

2. CARRIER. Ay, when? canst tell? Lend me thy lantern, quoth he? Marry, I'll see thee hang'd first!

GADSHILL. Sirrah carrier, what time do you mean to come to London?

2. CARRIER. Time enough to go to bed with a candle, I warrant thee. Come, neighbour Mugs, we'll call up the gentlemen. They will along with company, for they have great charge. *Exeunt CARRIERS*

GADSHILL. What, ho! chamberlain!

Enter CHAMBERLAIN

CHAMBERLAIN. At hand, quoth pickpurse.

GADSHILL. That's even as fair as- 'at hand, quoth the chamberlain'; for thou variest no more from picking of purses than giving direction doth from labouring: thou layest the plot how.

CHAMBERLAIN. Good morrow, Master Gadshill. It

holds current that I told you yesternight. There's a franklin in the Wild of Kent hath brought three hundred marks with him in gold. I heard him tell it to one of his company last night at supper- a kind of auditor; one that hath abundance of charge too, God knows what. They are up already and call for eggs and butter. They will away presently.

GADSHILL. Sirrah, if they meet not with Saint Nicholas' clerks, I'll give thee this neck.

CHAMBERLAIN. No, I'll none of it. I pray thee keep that for the hangman; for I know thou worshippest Saint Nicholas as truly as a man of falsehood may.

GADSHILL. What talkest thou to me of the hangman? If I hang, I'll make a fat pair of gallows; for if I hang, old Sir John hangs with me, and thou knowest he is no starveling. Tut! there are other Troyans that thou dream'st not of, the which for sport sake are content to do the profession some grace; that would (if matters should be look'd into) for their own credit sake make all whole. I am joined with no foot land-rakers, no long-staff sixpenny strikers, none of these mad mustachio purple-hued maltworms; but with nobility, and tranquillity, burgomasters and great oneyers, such as can hold in, such as will strike sooner than speak, and speak sooner than drink, and drink sooner than pray; and yet, zounds, I lie; for they pray continually to their saint, the commonwealth, or rather, not pray to her, but prey on her, for they ride up and down on her and make her their boots.

CHAMBERLAIN. What, the commonwealth their boots? Will she hold out water in foul way?

GADSHILL. She will, she will! Justice hath liquor'd her. We steal as in a castle, cocksure. We have the receipt of fernseed, we walk invisible.

CHAMBERLAIN. Nay, by my faith, I think you are more beholding to the night than to fernseed for your walking invisible.

GADSHILL. Give me thy hand. Thou shalt have a share in our purchase, as I and a true man.

CHAMBERLAIN. Nay, rather let me have it, as you are a false thief.

GADSHILL. Go to; 'homo' is a common name to all men. Bid the ostler bring my gelding out of the stable. Farewell, you muddy knave.   *Exeunt*

SCENE II

The highway near Gadshill

Enter PRINCE and POINS

POINS. Come, shelter, shelter! I have remov'd Falstaff's horse, and he frets like a gumm'd velvet.

PRINCE. Stand close. *[They step aside]*

Enter FALSTAFF

FALSTAFF. Poins! Poins, and be hang'd! Poins!

PRINCE. I comes forward I Peace, ye fat-kidney'd rascal! What a brawling dost thou keep!

FALSTAFF. Where's Poins, Hal?

PRINCE. He is walk'd up to the top of the hill. I'll go seek him. *[Steps aside]*

FALSTAFF. I am accurs'd to rob in that thief's company. The rascal hath removed my horse and tied him I know not where. If I travel but four foot by the squire further afoot, I shall break my wind. Well, I doubt not but to die a fair death for all this, if I scape hanging for killing that rogue. I have forsworn his company hourly any time this two-and-twenty years, and yet I am bewitch'd with the rogue's company. If the rascal have not given me medicines to make me love him, I'll be hang'd. It could not be else. I have drunk medicines. Poins! Hal! A plague upon you both! Bardolph! Peto! I'll starve ere I'll rob a foot further. An 'twere not as good a deed as drink to turn true man and to leave these rogues, I am the veriest varlet that ever chewed with a tooth. Eight yards of uneven ground is threescore and ten miles afoot with me, and the stony-hearted villains know it well enough. A plague upon it when thieves cannot be true one to another! (They whistle.) Whew! A plague upon you all! Give me my horse, you rogues! give me my horse and be hang'd!

PRINCE. *[Comes forward]* Peace, ye fat-guts! Lie down, lay thine ear close to the ground, and list if thou canst hear the tread of travellers.

FALSTAFF. Have you any levers to lift me up again, being down? 'Sblood, I'll not bear mine own flesh so far afoot again for all the coin in thy father's exchequer. What a plague mean ye to colt me thus?

PRINCE. Thou liest; thou art not colted, thou art uncolted.

FALSTAFF. I prithee, good Prince Hal, help me to my horse, good king's son.

PRINCE. Out, ye rogue! Shall I be your ostler?

FALSTAFF. Go hang thyself in thine own heir-apparent garters! If I be ta'en, I'll peach for this. An I have not ballads made on you all, and sung to filthy tunes, let a cup of sack be my poison. When a jest is so forward- and afoot too- I hate it.

Enter GADSHILL, BARDOLPH and PETO with him

GADSHILL. Stand!

FALSTAFF. So I do, against my will.

POINS. *[Comes fortward]* O, 'tis our setter. I know his voice. Bardolph, what news?

BARDOLPH. Case ye, case ye! On with your vizards! There's money of the King's coming down the hill; 'tis going to the King's exchequer.

FALSTAFF. You lie, ye rogue! 'Tis going to the King's tavern.

GADSHILL. There's enough to make us all.

FALSTAFF. To be hang'd.

PRINCE. Sirs, you four shall front them in the narrow lane; Ned Poins and I will walk lower. If they scape from your encounter, then they light on us.

PETO. How many be there of them?

GADSHILL. Some eight or ten.

FALSTAFF. Zounds, will they not rob us?

PRINCE. What, a coward, Sir John Paunch?

FALSTAFF. Indeed, I am not John of Gaunt, your grandfather; but yet no coward, Hal.

PRINCE. Well, we leave that to the proof.

POINS. Sirrah Jack, thy horse stands behind the hedge. When thou need'st him, there thou shalt find him. Farewell and stand fast.

FALSTAFF. Now cannot I strike him, if I should be hang'd.

PRINCE. *[Aside to POINS]* Ned, where are our disguises?

POINS. *[Aside to PRINCE]* Here, hard by. Stand close.
Exeunt PRINCE and POINS

FALSTAFF. Now, my masters, happy man be his dole, say I. Every man to his business.

Enter the TRAVELLERS

TRAVELLER. Come, neighbour. The boy shall lead our horses down the hill; We'll walk afoot awhile and ease our legs.

THIEVES. Stand!

TRAVELLER. Jesus bless us!

FALSTAFF. Strike! down with them! cut the villains' throats! Ah, whoreson caterpillars! bacon-fed knaves! they hate us youth. Down with them! fleece them!

TRAVELLER. O, we are undone, both we and ours for ever!

FALSTAFF. Hang ye, gorbellied knaves, are ye undone? No, ye fat chuffs; I would your store were here! On, bacons on! What, ye knaves! young men must live. You are grandjurors, are ye? We'll jure ye, faith! *[Here they rob and bind them]* *Exeunt*

Enter the PRINCE and POINS in buckram suits

PRINCE. The thieves have bound the true men. Now could thou and I rob the thieves and go merrily to London, it would be argument for a week, laughter for a month, and a good jest for ever.

POINS. Stand close! I hear them coming.
[They stand aside]

Enter the THIEVES again

FALSTAFF. Come, my masters, let us share, and then to horse before day. An the Prince and Poins be not two arrant cowards, there's no equity stirring. There's no more valour in that Poins than in a wild duck.

[As they are sharing, the Prince and Poins set upon them. They all run away, and Falstaff, after a blow or two, runs

awasy too, leaving the booty behind them.]

PRINCE. Your money!

POINS. Villains!

PRINCE. Got with much ease. Now merrily to horse.
The thieves are scattered, and possess'd with fear
So strongly that they dare not meet each other.
Each takes his fellow for an officer.
Away, good Ned. Falstaff sweats to death
And lards the lean earth as he walks along.
Were't not for laughing, I should pity him.

POINS. How the rogue roar'd!   *Exeunt*

SCENE III

Warkworth Castle

Enter HOTSPUR solus, reading a letter

HOTSPUR. 'But, for mine own part, my lord, I could be
well contented to be there, in respect of the love I bear
your house.' He could be contented- why is he not then?
In respect of the love he bears our house! He shows in this
he loves his own barn better than he loves our house. Let
me see some more. 'The purpose you undertake is dangerous'- Why, that's certain! 'Tis dangerous to take a cold,
to sleep, to drink; but I tell you, my lord fool, out of this
nettle, danger, we pluck this flower, safety. 'The purpose
you undertake is dangerous, the friends you have named
uncertain, the time itself unsorted, and your whole plot
too light for the counterpoise of so great an opposition.'
Say you so, say you so? I say unto you again, you are a
shallow, cowardly hind, and you lie. What a lack-brain is
this! By the Lord, our plot is a good plot as ever was laid;
our friends true and constant: a good plot, good friends,
and full of expectation; an excellent plot, very good

friends. What a frosty-spirited rogue is this! Why, my Lord of York commends the plot and the general course of the action. Zounds, an I were now by this rascal, I could brain him with his lady's fan. Is there not my father, my uncle, and myself; Lord Edmund Mortimer, my Lord of York, and Owen Glendower? Is there not, besides, the Douglas? Have I not all their letters to meet me in arms by the ninth of the next month, and are they not some of them set forward already? What a pagan rascal is this! an infidel! Ha! you shall see now, in very sincerity of fear and cold heart will he to the King and lay open all our proceedings. O, I could divide myself and go to buffets for moving such a dish of skim milk with so honourable an action! Hang him, let him tell the King! we are prepared. I will set forward to-night.

Enter his LADY

How now, Kate? I must leave you within these two hours.

LADY. O my good lord, why are you thus alone?
For what offence have I this fortnight been
A banish'd woman from my Harry's bed,
Tell me, sweet lord, what is't that takes from thee
Thy stomach, pleasure, and thy golden sleep?
Why dost thou bend thine eyes upon the earth,
And start so often when thou sit'st alone?
Why hast thou lost the fresh blood in thy cheeks
And given my treasures and my rights of thee
To thick-ey'd musing and curs'd melancholy?
In thy faint slumbers I by thee have watch'd,
And heard thee murmur tales of iron wars,
Speak terms of manage to thy bounding steed,
Cry 'Courage! to the field!' And thou hast talk'd
Of sallies and retires, of trenches, tent,
Of palisadoes, frontiers, parapets,
Of basilisks, of cannon, culverin,

Of prisoners' ransom, and of soldiers slain,
And all the currents of a heady fight.
Thy spirit within thee hath been so at war,
And thus hath so bestirr'd thee in thy sleep,
That beads of sweat have stood upon thy brow
Like bubbles ill a late-disturbed stream,
And in thy face strange motions have appear'd,
Such as we see when men restrain their breath
On some great sudden hest. O, what portents are these?
Some heavy business hath my lord in hand,
And I must know it, else he loves me not.

HOTSPUR. What, ho!

Enter a SERVANT

Is Gilliams with the packet gone?

SERVANT. He is, my lord, an hour ago.

HOTSPUR. Hath Butler brought those horses from the sheriff?

SERVANT. One horse, my lord, he brought even now.

HOTSPUR. What horse? A roan, a crop-ear, is it not?

SERVANT. It is, my lord.

HOTSPUR. That roan shall be my throne.
Well, I will back him straight. O esperance!
Bid Butler lead him forth into the park. *Exit SERVANT*

LADY. But hear you, my lord.

HOTSPUR. What say'st thou, my lady?

LADY. What is it carries you away?

HOTSPUR. Why, my horse, my love- my horse!

LADY. Out, you mad-headed ape!
A weasel hath not such a deal of spleen
As you are toss'd with. In faith,

I'll know your business, Harry; that I will!
I fear my brother Mortimer doth stir
About his title and hath sent for you
To line his enterprise; but if you go-

HOTSPUR. So far afoot, I shall be weary, love.

LADY. Come, come, you paraquito, answer me
Directly unto this question that I ask.
I'll break thy little finger, Harry,
An if thou wilt not tell my all things true.

HOTSPUR. Away.
Away, you trifler! Love? I love thee not;
I care not for thee, Kate. This is no world
To play with mammets and to tilt with lips.
We must have bloody noses and crack'd crowns,
And pass them current too. Gods me, my horse!
What say'st thou, Kate? What wouldst thou have with
me?

LADY. Do you not love me? do you not indeed?
Well, do not then; for since you love me not,
I will not love myself. Do you not love me?
Nay, tell me if you speak in jest or no.

HOTSPUR. Come, wilt thou see me ride?
And when I am a-horseback, I will swear
I love thee infinitely. But hark you. Kate:
I must not have you henceforth question me
Whither I go, nor reason whereabout.
Whither I must, I must; and to conclude,
This evening must I leave you, gentle Kate.
I know you wise; but yet no farther wise
Than Harry Percy's wife; constant you are,
But yet a woman; and for secrecy,
No lady closer, for I well believe
Thou wilt not utter what thou dost not know,
And so far will I trust thee, gentle Kate.

LADY. How? so far?

HOTSPUR. Not an inch further. But hark you, Kate:
Whither I go, thither shall you go too;
To-day will I set forth, to-morrow you.
Will this content you, Kate,?

LADY. It must of force.   *Exeunt*

SCENE IV

Eastcheap. The Boar's Head Tavern

Enter PRINCE and POINS

PRINCE. Ned, prithee come out of that fat-room and
lend me thy hand to laugh a little.

POINS. Where hast been, Hal?

PRINCE,. With three or four loggerheads amongst three
or fourscore hogsheads. I have sounded the very bass-
string of humility. Sirrah, I am sworn brother to a leash
of drawers and can call them all by their christen names,
as Tom, Dick, and Francis. They take it already upon
their salvation that, though I be but Prince of Wales, yet
I am the king of courtesy; and tell me flatly I am no
proud Jack like Falstaff, but a Corinthian, a lad of mettle,
a good boy (by the Lord, so they call me!), and when I am
King of England I shall command all the good lads
Eastcheap. They call drinking deep, dying scarlet; and
when you breathe in your watering, they cry 'hem!' and
bid you play it off. To conclude, I am so good a proficient
in one quarter of an hour that I can drink with any tin-
ker in his own language during my life. I tell thee, Ned,
thou hast lost much honour that thou wert not with me
in this action. But, sweet Ned- to sweeten which name of
Ned, I give thee this pennyworth of sugar, clapp'd even
now into my hand by an under-skinker, one that never
spake other English in his life than 'Eight shillings and
sixpence,' and 'You are welcome,' with this shrill

addition, 'Anon, anon, sir! Score a pint of bastard in the Half-moon,' or so- but, Ned, to drive away the time till Falstaff come, I prithee do thou stand in some by-room while I question my puny drawer to what end be gave me the sugar; and do thou never leave calling 'Francis!' that his tale to me may be nothing but 'Anon!' Step aside, and I'll show thee a precedent.

POINS. Francis!

PRINCE. Thou art perfect.

POINS. Francis! *Exit POINS*

Enter FRANCIS, a Drawer

FRANCIS. Anon, anon, sir.- Look down into the Pomgarnet, Ralph.

PRINCE. Come hither, Francis.

FRANCIS. My lord?

PRINCE. How long hast thou to serve, Francis?

FRANCIS. Forsooth, five years, and as much as to-

POINS. [*Within*] Francis!

FRANCIS. Anon, anon, sir.

PRINCE. Five year! by'r Lady, a long lease for the clinking of Pewter. But, Francis, darest thou be so valiant as to play the coward with thy indenture and show it a fair pair of heels and run from it?

FRANCIS. O Lord, sir, I'll be sworn upon all the books in England I could find in my heart-

POINS. [*Within*] Francis!

FRANCIS. Anon, sir.

PRINCE. How old art thou, Francis?

FRANCIS. Let me see. About Michaelmas next I

shall be-

POINS. *[Within]* Francis!

FRANCIS. Anon, sir. Pray stay a little, my lord.

PRINCE. Nay, but hark you, Francis. For the sugar thou gavest me- 'twas a pennyworth, wast not?

FRANCIS. O Lord! I would it had been two!

PRINCE. I will give thee for it a thousand pound. Ask me when thou wilt, and, thou shalt have it.

POINS. *[Within]* Francis!

FRANCIS. Anon, anon.

PRINCE. Anon, Francis? No, Francis; but to-morrow, Francis; or, Francis, a Thursday; or indeed, Francis, when thou wilt. But Francis-

FRANCIS. My lord?

PRINCE. Wilt thou rob this leathern-jerkin, crystal-button, not-pated, agate-ring, puke-stocking, caddis-garter, smooth-tongue, Spanish-pouch-

FRANCIS. O Lord, sir, who do you mean?

PRINCE. Why then, your brown bastard is your only drink; for look you, Francis, your white canvas doublet will sully. In Barbary, sir, it cannot come to so much.

FRANCIS. What, sir?

POINS. *[Within]* Francis!

PRINCE. Away, you rogue! Dost thou not hear them call? *[Here they both call him. The Drawer stands amazed, not knowing which way to go.]*

Enter VINTNER

VINTNER. What, stand'st thou still, and hear'st such a calling? Look to the guests within. *[Exit Francis]*

My lord, old Sir John, with half-a-dozen more, are at the door. Shall I let them in?

PRINCE. Let them alone awhile, and then open the door. *Exit VINTNER*

Poins!

POINS. *[Within]* Anon, anon, sir.

Enter POINS

PRINCE. Sirrah, Falstaff and the rest of the thieves are at the door. Shall we be merry?

POINS. As merry as crickets, my lad. But hark ye; what cunning match have you made with this jest of the drawer? Come, what's the issue?

PRINCE. I am now of all humours that have showed themselves humours since the old days of goodman Adam to the pupil age of this present this twelve o'clock at midnight.

Enter FRANCIS

What's o'clock, Francis?

FRANCIS. Anon, anon, sir. *Exit*

PRINCE. That ever this fellow should have fewer words than a parrot, and yet the son of a woman! His industry is upstairs and downstairs, his eloquence the parcel of a reckoning. I am not yet of Percy's mind, the Hotspur of the North; he that kills me some six or seven dozen of Scots at a breakfast, washes his hands, and says to his wife, 'Fie upon this quiet life! I want work.' 'O my sweet Harry,' says she, 'how many hast thou kill'd to-day?' 'Give my roan horse a drench,' says he, and answers 'Some fourteen,' an hour after, 'a trifle, a trifle.' I prithee call in Falstaff. I'll play Percy, and that damn'd brawn shall play Dame Mortimer his wife. 'Rivo!' says the drunkard. Call in ribs, call in tallow.

*Enter FALSTAFF, GADSHILL, BARDOLPH, and
PETO; FRANCIS follows with wine*

POINS. Welcome, Jack. Where hast thou been?

FALSTAFF. A plague of all cowards, I say, and a
vengeance too! Marry and amen! Give me a cup of sack,
boy. Ere I lead this life long, I'll sew nether-stocks, and
mend them and foot them too. A plague of all cowards!
Give me a cup of sack, rogue. Is there no virtue extant?

[He drinketh]

PRINCE. Didst thou never see Titan kiss a dish of butter? Pitiful-hearted butter, that melted at the sweet tale of
the sun! If thou didst, then behold that compound.

FALSTAFF. You rogue, here's lime in this sack too! There
is nothing but roguery to be found in villanous man. Yet
a coward is worse than a cup of sack with lime in it- a villanous coward! Go thy ways, old Jack, die when thou
wilt; if manhood, good manhood, be not forgot upon the
face of the earth, then am I a shotten herring. There lives
not three good men unhang'd in England; and one of
them is fat, and grows old. God help the while! A bad
world, I say. I would I were a weaver; I could sing psalms
or anything. A plague of all cowards I say still!

PRINCE. How now, woolsack? What mutter you?

FALSTAFF. A king's son! If I do not beat thee out of thy
kingdom with a dagger of lath and drive all thy subjects
afore thee like a flock of wild geese, I'll never wear hair on
my face more. You Prince of Wales?

PRINCE. Why, you whoreson round man, what's the
matter?

FALSTAFF. Are not you a coward? Answer me to
that- and Poins there?

POINS. Zounds, ye fat paunch, an ye call me coward, by the Lord, I'll stab thee.

FALSTAFF. I call thee coward? I'll see thee damn'd ere I call thee coward, but I would give a thousand pound I could run as fast as thou canst. You are straight enough in the shoulders; you care not who sees Your back. Call you that backing of your friends? A plague upon such backing! Give me them that will face me. Give me a cup of sack. I am a rogue if I drunk to-day.

PRINCE. O villain! thy lips are scarce wip'd since thou drunk'st last.

FALSTAFF. All is one for that. [He drinketh] A plague of all cowards still say I.

PRINCE. What's the matter?

FALSTAFF. What's the matter? There be four of us here have ta'en a thousand pound this day morning.

PRINCE. Where is it, Jack? Where is it?

FALSTAFF. Where is it, Taken from us it is. A hundred upon poor four of us!

PRINCE. What, a hundred, man?

FALSTAFF. I am a rogue if I were not at half-sword with a dozen of them two hours together. I have scap'd by miracle. I am eight times thrust through the doublet, four through the hose; my buckler cut through and through; my sword hack'd like a handsaw- ecce signum! I never dealt better since I was a man. All would not do. A plague of all cowards! Let them speak, If they speak more or less than truth, they are villains and the sons of darkness.

PRINCE. Speak, sirs. How was it?

GADSHILL. We four set upon some dozen-

FALSTAFF. Sixteen at least, my lord.

GADSHILL. And bound them.

PETO. No, no, they were not bound.

FALSTAFF. You rogue, they were bound, every man of them, or I am a Jew else- an Ebrew Jew.

GADSHILL. As we were sharing, some six or seven fresh men sea upon us-

FALSTAFF. And unbound the rest, and then come in the other.

PRINCE. What, fought you with them all?

FALSTAFF. All? I know not what you call all, but if I fought not with fifty of them, I am a bunch of radish! If there were not two or three and fifty upon poor old Jack, then am I no two-legg'd creature.

PRINCE. Pray God you have not murd'red some of them.

FALSTAFF. Nay, that's past praying for. I have pepper'd two of them. Two I am sure I have paid, two rogues in buckram suits. I tell thee what, Hal- if I tell thee a lie, spit in my face, call me horse. Thou knowest my old ward. Here I lay, and thus I bore my point. Four rogues in buckram let drive at me.

PRINCE. What, four? Thou saidst but two even now.

FALSTAFF. Four, Hal. I told thee four.

POINS. Ay, ay, he said four.

FALSTAFF. These four came all afront and mainly thrust at me. I made me no more ado but took all their seven points in my target, thus.

PRINCE. Seven? Why, there were but four even now.

FALSTAFF. In buckram?

POINS. Ay, four, in buckram suits.

FALSTAFF. Seven, by these hilts, or I am a villain else.

PRINCE. *[Aside to POINS]* Prithee let him alone. We

shall have more anon.

FALSTAFF. Dost thou hear me, Hal?

PRINCE. Ay, and mark thee too, Jack.

FALSTAFF. Do so, for it is worth the list'ning to. These nine in buckram that I told thee of-

PRINCE. So, two more already.

FALSTAFF. Their points being broken-

POINS. Down fell their hose.

FALSTAFF. Began to give me ground; but I followed me close, came in, foot and hand, and with a thought seven of the eleven I paid.

PRINCE. O monstrous! Eleven buckram men grown out of two!

FALSTAFF. But, as the devil would have it, three misbegotten knaves in Kendal green came at my back and let drive at me; for it was so dark, Hal, that thou couldst not see thy hand.

PRINCE. These lies are like their father that begets them-gross as a mountain, open, palpable. Why, thou clay-brain'd guts, thou knotty-pated fool, thou whoreson obscene greasy tallow-catch-

FALSTAFF. What, art thou mad? art thou mad? Is not the truth the truth?

PRINCE. Why, how couldst thou know these men in Kendal green when it was so dark thou couldst not see thy hand? Come, tell us your reason. What sayest thou to this?

POINS. Come, your reason, Jack, your reason.

FALSTAFF. What, upon compulsion? Zounds, an I were at the strappado or all the racks in the world, I would not tell you on compulsion. Give you a reason on compulsion? If reasons were as plentiful as blackberries, I would give no man a reason upon compulsion, I.

PRINCE. I'll be no longer guilty, of this sin; this sanguine coward, this bed-presser, this horseback-breaker, this huge hill of flesh-

FALSTAFF. 'Sblood, you starveling, you elf-skin, you dried neat's-tongue, you bull's sizzle, you stockfish- O for breath to utter what is like thee!- you tailor's yard, you sheath, you bowcase, you vile standing tuck!

PRINCE. Well, breathe awhile, and then to it again; and when thou hast tired thyself in base comparisons, hear me speak but this.

POINS. Mark, Jack.

PRINCE. We two saw you four set on four, and bound them and were masters of their wealth. Mark now how a plain tale shall put you down. Then did we two set on you four and, with a word, outfac'd you from your prize, and have it; yea, and can show it you here in the house. And, Falstaff, you carried your guts away as nimbly, with as quick dexterity, and roar'd for mercy, and still run and roar'd, as ever I heard bullcalf. What a slave art thou to hack thy sword as thou hast done, and then say it was in fight! What trick, what device, what starting hole canst thou now find out to hide thee from this open and apparent shame?

POINS. Come, let's hear, Jack. What trick hast thou now?

FALSTAFF. By the Lord, I knew ye as well as he that made ye. Why, hear you, my masters. Was it for me to kill the heir apparent? Should I turn upon the true prince? Why, thou knowest I am as valiant as Hercules; but beware instinct. The lion will not touch the true prince. Instinct is a great matter. I was now a coward on instinct. I shall think the better of myself, and thee, during my life- I for a valiant lion, and thou for a true prince. But, by the Lord, lads, I am glad you have the money. Hostess, clap to the doors. Watch to-night, pray to-morrow. Gallants, lads, boys, hearts of gold, all the titles of good fellowship come to you! What, shall we be merry? Shall we have a play extempore?

PRINCE. Content- and the argument shall be thy running away.

FALSTAFF. Ah, no more of that, Hal, an thou lovest me!

Enter HOSTESS

HOSTESS. O Jesu, my lord the Prince!

PRINCE. How now, my lady the hostess? What say'st thou to me?

HOSTESS. Marry, my lord, there is a nobleman of the court at door would speak with you. He says he comes from your father.

PRINCE. Give him as much as will make him a royal man, and send him back again to my mother.

FALSTAFF. What manner of man is he?

HOSTESS. An old man.

FALSTAFF. What doth gravity out of his bed at midnight? Shall I give him his answer?

PRINCE. Prithee do, Jack.

FALSTAFF. Faith, and I'll send him packing.   *Exit*

PRINCE. Now, sirs. By'r Lady, you fought fair; so did you, Peto; so did you, Bardolph. You are lions too, you ran away upon instinct,   you will not touch the true prince; no- fie!

BARDOLPH. Faith, I ran when I saw others run.

PRINCE. Tell me now in earnest, how came Falstaff's sword so hack'd?

PETO. Why, he hack'd it with his dagger, and said he would swear truth out of England but he would make you believe it was done in fight, and persuaded us to do the like.

BARDOLPH. Yea, and to tickle our noses with spear-grass to make them bleed, and then to beslubber our garments with it and swear it was the blood of true men. I did that I did not this seven year before- I blush'd to hear his monstrous devices.

PRINCE. O villain! thou stolest a cup of sack eighteen years ago and wert taken with the manner, and ever since thou hast blush'd extempore. Thou hadst fire and sword on thy side, and yet thou ran'st away. What instinct hadst thou for it?

BARDOLPH. My lord, do you see these meteors? Do you behold these exhalations?

PRINCE. I do.

BARDOLPH. What think you they portend?

PRINCE. Hot livers and cold purses.

BARDOLPH. Choler, my lord, if rightly taken.

PRINCE. No, if rightly taken, halter.

Enter FALSTAFF

Here comes lean Jack; here comes bare-bone. How now, my sweet creature of bombast? How long is't ago, Jack, since thou sawest thine own knee?

FALSTAFF. My own knee? When I was about thy years, Hal, I was not an eagle's talent in the waist; I could have crept into any alderman's thumb-ring. A plague of sighing and grief! It blows a man up like a bladder. There's villanous news abroad. Here was Sir John Bracy from your father. You must to the court in the morning. That same mad fellow of the North, Percy, and he of Wales that gave Amamon the bastinado, and made Lucifer cuckold, and swore the devil his true liegeman upon the cross of a Welsh hook- what a plague call you him?

POINS. O, Glendower.

FALSTAFF. Owen, Owen- the same; and his son-in-law Mortimer, and old Northumberland, and that sprightly Scot of Scots, Douglas, that runs a-horseback up a hill perpendicular-

PRINCE. He that rides at high speed and with his pistol kills a sparrow flying.

FALSTAFF. You have hit it.

PRINCE. So did he never the sparrow.

FALSTAFF. Well, that rascal hath good metal in him; he will not run.

PRINCE. Why, what a rascal art thou then, to praise him so for running!

FALSTAFF. A-horseback, ye cuckoo! but afoot he will not budge a foot.

PRINCE. Yes, Jack, upon instinct.

FALSTAFF. I grant ye, upon instinct. Well, he is there too, and one Mordake, and a thousand bluecaps more. Worcester is stol'n away to-night; thy father's beard is turn'd white with the news; you may buy land now as cheap as stinking mack'rel.

PRINCE. Why then, it is like, if there come a hot June, and this civil buffeting hold, we shall buy maidenheads as they buy hobnails, by the hundreds.

FALSTAFF. By the mass, lad, thou sayest true; it is like we shall have good trading that way. But tell me, Hal, art not thou horrible afeard? Thou being heir apparent, could the world pick thee out three such enemies again as that fiend Douglas, that spirit Percy, and that devil Glendower? Art thou not horribly afraid? Doth not thy blood thrill at it?

PRINCE. Not a whit, i' faith. I lack some of thy instinct.

FALSTAFF. Well, thou wilt be horribly chid to-morrow when thou comest to thy father. If thou love file, practise an answer.

PRINCE. Do thou stand for my father and examine me upon the particulars of my life.

FALSTAFF. Shall I? Content. This chair shall be my state, this dagger my sceptre, and this cushion my, crown.

PRINCE. Thy state is taken for a join'd-stool, thy golden sceptre for a leaden dagger, and thy precious rich crown for a pitiful bald crown.

FALSTAFF. Well, an the fire of grace be not quite out of thee, now shalt thou be moved. Give me a cup of sack to make my eyes look red, that it may be thought I have wept; for I must speak in passion, and I will do it in King Cambyses' vein.

PRINCE. Well, here is my leg.

FALSTAFF. And here is my speech. Stand aside, nobility.

HOSTESS. O Jesu, this is excellent sport, i' faith!

FALSTAFF. Weep not, sweet queen, for trickling tears are vain.

HOSTESS. O, the Father, how he holds his countenance!

FALSTAFF. For God's sake, lords, convey my tristful queen!
For tears do stop the floodgates of her eyes.

HOSTESS. O Jesu, he doth it as like one of these harlotry players as ever I see!

FALSTAFF. Peace, good pintpot. Peace, good tickle-brain.- Harry, I do not only marvel where thou spendest thy time, but also how thou art accompanied.

For though the camomile, the more it is trodden on, the faster it grows, yet youth, the more it is wasted, the sooner it wears. That thou art my son I have partly thy mother's word, partly my own opinion, but chiefly a villanous trick of thine eye and a foolish hanging of thy nether lip that doth warrant me. If then thou be son to me, here lies the point: why, being son to me, art thou so pointed at? Shall the blessed sun of heaven prove a micher and eat blackberries? A question not to be ask'd. Shall the son of England prove a thief and take purses? A question to be ask'd. There is a thing, Harry, which thou hast often heard of, and it is known to many in our land by the name of pitch. This pitch, as ancient writers do report, doth defile; so doth the company thou keepest. For, Harry, now I do not speak to thee in drink, but in tears; not in pleasure, but in passion; not in words only, but in woes also: and yet there is a virtuous man whom I have often noted in thy company, but I know not his name.

PRINCE. What manner of man, an it like your Majesty?

FALSTAFF. A goodly portly man, i' faith, and a corpulent; of a cheerful look, a pleasing eye, and a most noble carriage; and, as I think, his age some fifty, or, by'r Lady, inclining to threescore; and now I remember me, his name is Falstaff. If that man should be lewdly, given, he deceiveth me; for, Harry, I see virtue in his looks. If then the tree may be known by the fruit, as the fruit by the tree, then, peremptorily I speak it, there is virtue in that Falstaff. Him keep with, the rest banish. And tell me now, thou naughty varlet, tell me where hast thou been this month?

PRINCE. Dost thou speak like a king? Do thou stand for me, and I'll play my father.

FALSTAFF. Depose me? If thou dost it half so gravely, so majestically, both in word and matter, hang me up by the heels for a rabbit-sucker or a poulter's hare.

William Shakespeare

PRINCE. Well, here I am set.

FALSTAFF. And here I stand. Judge, my masters.

PRINCE. Now, Harry, whence come you?

FALSTAFF. My noble lord, from Eastcheap.

PRINCE. The complaints I hear of thee are grievous.

FALSTAFF. 'Sblood, my lord, they are false! Nay, I'll tickle ye for a young prince, i' faith.

PRINCE. Swearest thou, ungracious boy? Henceforth ne'er look on me. Thou art violently carried away from grace. There is a devil haunts thee in the likeness of an old fat man; a tun of man is thy companion. Why dost thou converse with that trunk of humours, that bolting hutch of beastliness, that swoll'n parcel of dropsies, that huge bombard of sack, that stuff'd cloakbag of guts, that roasted Manningtree ox with the pudding in his belly, that reverend vice, that grey iniquity, that father ruffian, that vanity in years? Wherein is he good, but to taste sack and drink it? wherein neat and cleanly, but to carve a capon and eat it? wherein cunning, but in craft? wherein crafty, but in villany? wherein villanous, but in all things? wherein worthy, but in nothing?

FALSTAFF. I would your Grace would take me with you. Whom means your Grace?

PRINCE. That villanous abominable misleader of youth, Falstaff, that old white-bearded Satan.

FALSTAFF. My lord, the man I know.

PRINCE. I know thou dost.

FALSTAFF. But to say I know more harm in him than in myself were to say more than I know. That he is old (the more the pity) his white hairs do witness it; but that he is (saving your reverence) a whoremaster, that I utterly deny. If sack and sugar be a fault, God help the wicked! If to be old and merry be a sin, then many an old host that I know is damn'd. If to be fat be to be hated, then Pharaoh's lean kine are to be loved. No, my good lord. Banish Peto, banish Bardolph, banish Poins; but for sweet Jack Falstaff, kind Jack Falstaff, true Jack Falstaff, valiant Jack Falstaff, and therefore more valiant being, as he is, old Jack Falstaff, banish not him thy Harry's company, banish not him thy Harry's company. Banish plump Jack, and banish all the world!

PRINCE. I do, I will. *[A knocking heard]*
Exeunt HOSTESS, FRANCIS, and BARDOLPH

Enter BARDOLPH, running

BARDOLPH. O, my lord, my lord! the sheriff with a most monstrous watch is at the door.

FALSTAFF. Out, ye rogue! Play out the play. I have much to say in the behalf of that Falstaff.

Enter the HOSTESS

HOSTESS. O Jesu, my lord, my lord!

PRINCE. Heigh, heigh, the devil rides upon a fiddle-stick! What's the matter?

HOSTESS. The sheriff and all the watch are at the door. They are come to search the house. Shall I let them in?

FALSTAFF. Dost thou hear, Hal? Never call a true piece of gold a counterfeit. Thou art essentially mad without seeming so.

PRINCE. And thou a natural coward without instinct.

FALSTAFF. I deny your major. If you will deny the sheriff, so; if not, let him enter. If I become not a cart as well as another man, a plague on my bringing up! I hope I shall as soon be strangled with a halter as another.

PRINCE. Go hide thee behind the arras. The rest walk,

up above. Now, my masters, for a true face and good con-
science.

FALSTAFF. Both which I have had; but their date is out,
and therefore I'll hide me. *Exit*

PRINCE. Call in the sheriff.

Exeunt MANENT THE PRINCE and PETO

Enter SHERIFF and the CARRIER

Now, Master Sheriff, what is your will with me?

SHERIFF. First, pardon me, my lord. A hue and cry
Hath followed certain men unto this house.

PRINCE. What men?

SHERIFF. One of them is well known, my gracious lord-
A gross fat man.

CARRIER. As fat as butter.

PRINCE. The man, I do assure you, is not here,
For I myself at this time have employ'd him.
And, sheriff, I will engage my word to thee
That I will by to-morrow dinner time
Send him to answer thee, or any man,
For anything he shall be charg'd withal;
And so let me entreat you leave the house.

SHERIFF. I will, my lord. There are two gentlemen
Have in this robbery lost three hundred marks.

PRINCE. It may be so. If he have robb'd these men,
He shall be answerable; and so farewell.

SHERIFF. Good night, my noble lord.

PRINCE. I think it is good morrow, is it not?

SHERIFF. Indeed, my lord, I think it be two o'clock.
Exit with CARRIER

PRINCE. This oily rascal is known as well as Paul's. Go

call him forth.

PETO. Falstaff! Fast asleep behind the arras, and snorting like a horse.

PRINCE. Hark how hard he fetches breath. Search his pockets. *[He searcheth his pockets and findeth certain papers]* What hast thou found?

PETO. Nothing but papers, my lord.

PRINCE. Let's see whit they be. Read them.

PETO. *[Reads]*

'Item. A capon.................... ii s. ii d.
Item, Sauce...................... iiii d.
Item, Sack two gallons .... v s. viii d.
Item, Anchovies and sack after supper. . . ii s. vi d.
Item, Bread...................... .ob.'

PRINCE. O monstrous! but one halfpennyworth of bread to this intolerable deal of sack! What there is else, keep close; we'll read it at more advantage. There let him sleep till day. I'll to the court in the morning . We must all to the wars. and thy place shall be honourable. I'll procure this fat rogue a charge of foot; and I know, his death will be a march of twelve score. The money shall be paid back again with advantage. Be with me betimes in the morning, and so good morrow, Peto.

PETO. Good morrow, good my lord.   *Exeunt*

ACT III

SCENE I

Bangor. The Archdeacon's house

*Enter HOTSPUR, WORCESTER, LORD MORTIMER,
OWEN GLENDOWER*

MORTIMER. These promises are fair, the parties sure,
And our induction full of prosperous hope.

HOTSPUR. Lord Mortimer, and cousin Glendower,
Will you sit down?
And uncle Worcester. A plague upon it!
I have forgot the map.

GLENDOWER. No, here it is.
Sit, cousin Percy; sit, good cousin Hotspur,
For by that name as oft as Lancaster
Doth speak of you, his cheek looks pale, and with
A rising sigh he wisheth you in heaven.

HOTSPUR. And you in hell, as oft as he hears
Owen Glendower spoke of.

GLENDOWER. I cannot blame him. At my nativity
The front of heaven was full of fiery shapes
Of burning cressets, and at my birth
The frame and huge foundation of the earth
Shak'd like a coward.

HOTSPUR. Why, so it would have done at the same season, if your mother's cat had but kitten'd, though yourself had never been born.

GLENDOWER. I say the earth did shake when I was
born.

HOTSPUR. And I say the earth was not of my mind,
If you suppose as fearing you it shook.

GLENDOWER. The heavens were all on fire, the earth

did tremble.

HOTSPUR. O, then the earth shook to see the heavens on fire,
And not in fear of your nativity.
Diseased nature oftentimes breaks forth
In strange eruptions; oft the teeming earth
Is with a kind of colic pinch'd and vex'd
By the imprisoning of unruly wind
Within her womb, which, for enlargement striving,
Shakes the old beldame earth and topples down
Steeples and mossgrown towers. At your birth
Our grandam earth, having this distemp'rature,
In passion shook.

GLENDOWER. Cousin, of many men
I do not bear these crossings. Give me leave
To tell you once again that at my birth
The front of heaven was full of fiery shapes,
The goats ran from the mountains, and the herds
Were strangely clamorous to the frighted fields.
These signs have mark'd me extraordinary,
And all the courses of my life do show
I am not in the roll of common men.
Where is he living, clipp'd in with the sea
That chides the banks of England, Scotland, Wales,
Which calls me pupil or hath read to me?
And bring him out that is but woman's son
Can trace me in the tedious ways of art
And hold me pace in deep experiments.

HOTSPUR. I think there's no man speaks better Welsh.
I'll to dinner.

MORTIMER. Peace, cousin Percy; you will make him mad.

GLENDOWER. I can call spirits from the vasty deep.

HOTSPUR. Why, so can I, or so can any man;
But will they come when you do call for them?

GLENDOWER. Why, I can teach you, cousin, to command the devil.

HOTSPUR. And I can teach thee, coz, to shame the devil-
By telling truth. Tell truth and shame the devil.
If thou have power to raise him, bring him hither,
And I'll be sworn I have power to shame him hence.
O, while you live, tell truth and shame the devil!

MORTIMER. Come, come, no more of this unprofitable chat.

GLENDOWER. Three times hath Henry Bolingbroke made head
Against my power; thrice from the banks of Wye
And sandy-bottom'd Severn have I sent him
Bootless home and weather-beaten back.

HOTSPUR. Home without boots, and in foul weather too?
How scapes he agues, in the devil's name

GLENDOWER. Come, here's the map. Shall we divide our right
According to our threefold order ta'en?

MORTIMER. The Archdeacon hath divided it
Into three limits very equally.
England, from Trent and Severn hitherto,
By south and east is to my part assign'd;
All westward, Wales beyond the Severn shore,
And all the fertile land within that bound,
To Owen Glendower; and, dear coz, to you
The remnant northward lying off from Trent.
And our indentures tripartite are drawn;
Which being sealed interchangeably
(A business that this night may execute),
To-morrow, cousin Percy, you and I
And my good Lord of Worcester will set forth
To meet your father and the Scottish bower,

As is appointed us, at Shrewsbury.
My father Glendower is not ready yet,
Nor shall we need his help these fourteen days.
[To GLENDOWER] Within that space you may have drawn together
Your tenants, friends, and neighbouring gentlemen.

GLENDOWER. A shorter time shall send me to you, lords;
And in my conduct shall your ladies come,
From whom you now must steal and take no leave,
For there will be a world of water shed
Upon the parting of your wives and you.

HOTSPUR. Methinks my moiety, north from Burton here,
In quantity equals not one of yours.
See how this river comes me cranking in
And cuts me from the best of all my land
A huge half-moon, a monstrous cantle out.
I'll have the current ill this place damm'd up,
And here the smug and sliver Trent shall run
In a new channel fair and evenly.
It shall not wind with such a deep indent
To rob me of so rich a bottom here.

GLENDOWER. Not wind? It shall, it must! You see it doth.

MORTIMER. Yea, but
Mark how he bears his course, and runs me up
With like advantage on the other side,
Gelding the opposed continent as much
As on the other side it takes from you.

WORCESTER. Yea, but a little charge will trench him here
And on this north side win this cape of land;
And then he runs straight and even.

HOTSPUR. I'll have it so. A little charge will do it.

GLENDOWER. I will not have it alt'red.

HOTSPUR. Will not you?

GLENDOWER. No, nor you shall not.

HOTSPUR. Who shall say me nay?

GLENDOWER. No, that will I.

HOTSPUR. Let me not understand you then; speak it in
Welsh.

GLENDOWER. I can speak English, lord, as well as
you;
For I was train'd up in the English court,
Where, being but young, I framed to the harp
Many an English ditty lovely well,
And gave the tongue a helpful ornament-
A virtue that was never seen in you.

HOTSPUR. Marry,
And I am glad of it with all my heart!
I had rather be a kitten and cry mew
Than one of these same metre ballet-mongers.
I had rather hear a brazen canstick turn'd
Or a dry wheel grate on the axletree,
And that would set my teeth nothing on edge,
Nothing so much as mincing poetry.
'Tis like the forc'd gait of a shuffling nag,

GLENDOWER. Come, you shall have Trent turn'd.

HOTSPUR. I do not care. I'll give thrice so much land
To any well-deserving friend;
But in the way of bargain, mark ye me,
I'll cavil on the ninth part of a hair
Are the indentures drawn? Shall we be gone?

GLENDOWER. The moon shines fair; you may away
by night.
I'll haste the writer, and withal
Break with your wives of your departure hence.

I am afraid my daughter will run mad,
So much she doteth on her Mortimer.   *Exit*

MORTIMER. Fie, cousin Percy! how you cross my
father!

HOTSPUR. I cannot choose. Sometimes he angers me
With telling me of the moldwarp and the ant,
Of the dreamer Merlin and his prophecies,
And of a dragon and a finless fish,
A clip-wing'd griffin and a moulten raven,
A couching lion and a ramping cat,
And such a deal of skimble-skamble stuff
As puts me from my faith. I tell you what-
He held me last night at least nine hours
In reckoning up the several devils' names
That were his lackeys. I cried 'hum,' and 'Well, go to!'
But mark'd him not a word. O, he is as tedious
As a tired horse, a railing wife;
Worse than a smoky house. I had rather live
With cheese and garlic in a windmill far
Than feed on cates and have him talk to me
In any summer house in Christendom).

MORTIMER. In faith, he is a worthy gentleman,
Exceedingly well read, and profited
In strange concealments, valiant as a lion,
And wondrous affable, and as bountiful
As mines of India. Shall I tell you, cousin?
He holds your temper in a high respect
And curbs himself even of his natural scope
When you come 'cross his humour. Faith, he does.
I warrant you that man is not alive
Might so have tempted him as you have done
Without the taste of danger and reproof.
But do not use it oft, let me entreat you.

WORCESTER. In faith, my lord, you are too wilful-
blame,
And since your coming hither have done enough

To put him quite besides his patience.
You must needs learn, lord, to amend this fault.
Though sometimes it show greatness, courage, blood-
And that's the dearest grace it renders you-
Yet oftentimes it doth present harsh rage,
Defect of manners, want of government,
Pride, haughtiness, opinion, and disdain;
The least of which haunting a nobleman
Loseth men's hearts, and leaves behind a stain
Upon the beauty of all parts besides,
Beguiling them of commendation.

HOTSPUR. Well, I am school'd. Good manners be
your speed!
Here come our wives, and let us take our leave.

Enter GLENDOWER with the LADIES

MORTIMER. This is the deadly spite that angers me-
My wife can speak no English, I no Welsh.

GLENDOWER. My daughter weeps; she will not part
with you;
She'll be a soldier too, she'll to the wars.

MORTIMER. Good father, tell her that she and my
aunt Percy
Shall follow in your conduct speedily. *[Glendower speaks
to her in Welsh, and she answers him in the same]*

GLENDOWER. She is desperate here. A peevish self-
will'd harlotry, One that no persuasion can do good
upon. *[The Lady speaks in Welsh]*

MORTIMER. I understand thy looks. That pretty
Welsh
Which thou pourest down from these swelling heavens
I am too perfect in; and, but for shame,
In such a Barley should I answer thee. *[The Lady again
in Welsh]*

I understand thy kisses, and thou mine,
And that's a feeling disputation.
But I will never be a truant, love,
Till I have learnt thy language: for thy tongue
Makes Welsh as sweet as ditties highly penn'd,
Sung by a fair queen in a summer's bow'r,
With ravishing division, to her lute.

GLENDOWER. Nay, if you melt, then will she run mad.
[The Lady speaks again in Welsh]

MORTIMER. O, I am ignorance itself in this!

GLENDOWER. She bids you on the wanton rushes lay
you down
And rest your gentle head upon her lap,
And she will sing the song that pleaseth you
And on your eyelids crown the god of sleep,
Charming your blood with pleasing heaviness,
Making such difference 'twixt wake and sleep
As is the difference betwixt day and night
The hour before the heavenly-harness'd team
Begins his golden progress in the East.

MORTIMER. With all my heart I'll sit and hear her
sing.
By that time will our book, I think, be drawn.

GLENDOWER. Do so,
And those musicians that shall play to you
Hang in the air a thousand leagues from hence,
And straight they shall be here. Sit, and attend.

HOTSPUR. Come, Kate, thou art perfect in lying down.
Come, quick, quick, that I may lay my head in thy lap.

LADY PERCY. Go, ye giddy goose.*[The music plays]*

HOTSPUR. Now I perceive the devil understands
Welsh;
And 'tis no marvel, be is so humorous.
By'r Lady, he is a good musician.

LADY PERCY. Then should you be nothing but musical; for you are altogether govern'd by humours. Lie still, ye thief, and hear the lady sing in Welsh.

HOTSPUR. I had rather hear Lady, my brach, howl in Irish.

LADY PERCY. Wouldst thou have thy head broken?

HOTSPUR. No.

LADY PERCY. Then be still.

HOTSPUR. Neither! 'Tis a woman's fault.

LADY PERCY. Now God help thee!

HOTSPUR. To the Welsh lady's bed.

LADY PERCY. What's that?

HOTSPUR. Peace! she sings. *[Here the Lady sings a Welsh song]*
Come, Kate, I'll have your song too.

LADY PERCY. Not mine, in good sooth.

HOTSPUR. Not yours, in good sooth? Heart! you swear like a comfit-maker's wife. 'Not you, in good sooth!' and 'as true as I live!' and 'as God shall mend me!' and 'as sure as day!'
And givest such sarcenet surety for thy oaths
As if thou ne'er walk'st further than Finsbury.
Swear me, Kate, like a lady as thou art,
A good mouth-filling oath; and leave 'in sooth'
And such protest of pepper gingerbread
To velvet guards and Sunday citizens. Come, sing.

LADY PERCY. I will not sing.

HOTSPUR. 'Tis the next way to turn tailor or be red-breast-teacher. An the indentures be drawn, I'll away within these two hours; and so come in when ye will.

Exit

GLENDOWER. Come, come, Lord Mortimer. You are as slow
As hot Lord Percy is on fire to go.
By this our book is drawn; we'll but seal,
And then to horse immediately.

MORTIMER. With all my heart.   *Exeunt*

SCENE II

London. The Palace

Enter the KING, PRINCE OF WALES, and others

KING. Lords, give us leave. The Prince of Wales and I
Must have some private conference; but be near at hand,
For we shall presently have need of you.

         Exeunt LORDS

I know not whether God will have it so,
For some displeasing service I have done,
That, in his secret doom, out of my blood
He'll breed revengement and a scourge for me;
But thou dost in thy passages of life
Make me believe that thou art only mark'd
For the hot vengeance and the rod of heaven
To punish my mistreadings. Tell me else,
Could such inordinate and low desires,
Such poor, such bare, such lewd, such mean attempts,
Such barren pleasures, rude society,
As thou art match'd withal and grafted to,
Accompany the greatness of thy blood
And hold their level with thy princely heart?

PRINCE. So please your Majesty, I would I could
Quit all offences with as clear excuse
As well as I am doubtless I can purge
Myself of many I am charged withal.

Yet such extenuation let me beg
As, in reproof of many tales devis'd,
Which oft the ear of greatness needs must bear
By, smiling pickthanks and base newsmongers,
I may, for some things true wherein my youth
Hath faulty wand'red and irregular,
And pardon on lily true submission.

KING. God pardon thee! Yet let me wonder, Harry,
At thy affections, which do hold a wing,
Quite from the flight of all thy ancestors.
Thy place in Council thou hast rudely lost,
Which by thy younger brother is supplied,
And art almost an alien to the hearts
Of all the court and princes of my blood.
The hope and expectation of thy time
Is ruin'd, and the soul of every man
Prophetically do forethink thy fall.
Had I so lavish of my presence been,
So common-hackney'd in the eyes of men,
So stale and cheap to vulgar company,
Opinion, that did help me to the crown,
Had still kept loyal to possession
And left me in reputeless banishment,
A fellow of no mark nor likelihood.
By being seldom seen, I could not stir
But, like a comet, I Was wond'red at;
That men would tell their children, 'This is he!'
Others would say, 'Where? Which is Bolingbroke?'
And then I stole all courtesy from heaven,
And dress'd myself in such humility
That I did pluck allegiance from men's hearts,
Loud shouts and salutations from their mouths
Even in the presence of the crowned King.
Thus did I keep my person fresh and new,
My presence, like a robe pontifical,
Ne'er seen but wond'red at; and so my state,
Seldom but sumptuous, show'd like a feast

And won by rareness such solemnity.
The skipping King, he ambled up and down
With shallow jesters and rash bavin wits,
Soon kindled and soon burnt; carded his state;
Mingled his royalty with cap'ring fools;
Had his great name profaned with their scorns
And gave his countenance, against his name,
To laugh at gibing boys and stand the push
Of every beardless vain comparative;
Grew a companion to the common streets,
Enfeoff'd himself to popularity;
That, being dally swallowed by men's eyes,
They surfeited with honey and began
To loathe the taste of sweetness, whereof a little
More than a little is by much too much.
So, when he had occasion to be seen,
He was but as the cuckoo is in June,
Heard, not regarded- seen, but with such eyes
As, sick and blunted with community,
Afford no extraordinary gaze,
Such as is bent on unlike majesty
When it shines seldom in admiring eyes;
But rather drows'd and hung their eyelids down,
Slept in his face, and rend'red such aspect
As cloudy men use to their adversaries,
Being with his presence glutted, gorg'd, and full.
And in that very line, Harry, standest thou;
For thou hast lost thy princely privilege
With vile participation. Not an eye
But is aweary of thy common sight,
Save mine, which hath desir'd to see thee more;
Which now doth that I would not have it do-
Make blind itself with foolish tenderness.

PRINCE. I shall hereafter, my thrice-gracious lord,
Be more myself.

KING. For all the world,
As thou art to this hour, was Richard then

When I from France set foot at Ravenspurgh;
And even as I was then is Percy now.
Now, by my sceptre, and my soul to boot,
He hath more worthy interest to the state
Than thou, the shadow of succession;
For of no right, nor colour like to right,
He doth fill fields with harness in the realm,
Turns head against the lion's armed jaws,
And, Being no more in debt to years than thou,
Leads ancient lords and reverend Bishops on
To bloody battles and to bruising arms.
What never-dying honour hath he got
Against renowmed Douglas! whose high deeds,
Whose hot incursions and great name in arms
Holds from all soldiers chief majority
And military title capital
Through all the kingdoms that acknowledge Christ.
Thrice hath this Hotspur, Mars in swathling clothes,
This infant warrior, in his enterprises
Discomfited great Douglas; ta'en him once,
Enlarged him, and made a friend of him,
To fill the mouth of deep defiance up
And shake the peace and safety of our throne.
And what say you to this? Percy, Northumberland,
The Archbishop's Grace of York, Douglas, Mortimer
Capitulate against us and are up.
But wherefore do I tell these news to thee
Why, Harry, do I tell thee of my foes,
Which art my nearest and dearest enemy'
Thou that art like enough, through vassal fear,
Base inclination, and the start of spleen,
To fight against me under Percy's pay,
To dog his heels and curtsy at his frowns,
To show how much thou art degenerate.

PRINCE. Do not think so. You shall not find it so.
And God forgive them that so much have sway'd
Your Majesty's good thoughts away from me!

I will redeem all this on Percy's head
And, in the closing of some glorious day,
Be bold to tell you that I am your son,
When I will wear a garment all of blood,
And stain my favours in a bloody mask,
Which, wash'd away, shall scour my shame with it.
And that shall be the day, whene'er it lights,
That this same child of honour and renown,
This gallant Hotspur, this all-praised knight,
And your unthought of Harry chance to meet.
For every honour sitting on his helm,
Would they were multitudes, and on my head
My shames redoubled! For the time will come
That I shall make this Northern youth exchange
His glorious deeds for my indignities.
Percy is but my factor, good my lord,
To engross up glorious deeds on my behalf;
And I will call hall to so strict account
That he shall render every glory up,
Yea, even the slightest worship of his time,
Or I will tear the reckoning from his heart.
This in the name of God I promise here;
The which if he be pleas'd I shall perform,
I do beseech your Majesty may salve
The long-grown wounds of my intemperance.
If not, the end of life cancels all bands,
And I will die a hundred thousand deaths
Ere break the smallest parcel of this vow.

KING. A hundred thousand rebels die in this!
Thou shalt have charge and sovereign trust herein.

Enter BLUNT

How now, good Blunt? Thy looks are full of speed.

BLUNT. So hath the business that I come to speak of.
Lord Mortimer of Scotland hath sent word
That Douglas and the English rebels met

The eleventh of this month at Shrewsbury.
A mighty and a fearful head they are,
If promises be kept oil every hand,
As ever off'red foul play in a state.

KING. The Earl of Westmoreland set forth to-day;
With him my son, Lord John of Lancaster;
For this advertisement is five days old.
On Wednesday next, Harry, you shall set forward;
On Thursday we ourselves will march. Our meeting
Is Bridgenorth; and, Harry, you shall march
Through Gloucestershire; by which account,
Our business valued, some twelve days hence
Our general forces at Bridgenorth shall meet.
Our hands are full of business. Let's away.
Advantage feeds him fat while men delay.   *Exeunt*

SCENE III

Eastcheap. The Boar's Head Tavern

Enter FALSTAFF and BARDOLPH

FALSTAFF. Bardolph, am I not fall'n away vilely since
this last action? Do I not bate? Do I not dwindle? Why,
my skin hangs about me like an old lady's loose gown! I
am withered like an old apple John. Well, I'll repent, and
that suddenly, while I am in some liking. I shall be out of
heart shortly, and then I shall have no strength to repent.
An I have not forgotten what the inside of a church is
made of, I am a peppercorn, a brewer's horse. The inside
of a church! Company, villanous company, hath been the
spoil of me.

BARDOLPH. Sir John, you are so fretful you cannot live
long.

FALSTAFF. Why, there is it! Come, sing me a bawdy
song; make me merry. I was as virtuously given as a

gentleman need to be, virtuous enough: swore little, dic'd not above seven times a week, went to a bawdy house not above once in a quarter- of an hour, paid money that I borrowed- three or four times, lived well, and in good compass; and now I live out of all order, out of all compass.

BARDOLPH. Why, you are so fat, Sir John, that you must needs be out of all compass- out of all reasonable compass, Sir John.

FALSTAFF. Do thou amend thy face, and I'll amend my life. Thou art our admiral, thou bearest the lantern in the poop- but 'tis in the nose of thee. Thou art the Knight of the Burning Lamp.

BARDOLPH. Why, Sir John, my face does you no harm.

FALSTAFF. No, I'll be sworn. I make as good use of it as many a man doth of a death's-head or a memento mori. I never see thy face but I think upon hellfire and Dives that lived in purple; for there he is in his robes, burning, burning. if thou wert any way given to virtue, I would swear by thy face; my oath should be 'By this fire, that's God's angel.' But thou art altogether given over, and wert indeed, but for the light in thy face, the son of utter darkness. When thou ran'st up Gadshill in the night to catch my horse, if I did not think thou hadst been an ignis fatuus or a ball of wildfire, there's no purchase in money. O, thou art a perpetual triumph, an everlasting bonfire-light! Thou hast saved me a thousand marks in links and torches, walking with thee in the night betwixt tavern and tavern; but the sack that thou hast drunk me would have bought me lights as good cheap at the dearest chandler's in Europe. I have maintained that salamander of yours with fire any time this two-and-thirty years. God reward me for it!

BARDOLPH. 'Sblood, I would my face were in your belly!

FALSTAFF. God-a-mercy! so should I be sure to be heart-burn'd.

Enter HOSTESS

How now, Dame Partlet the hen? Have you enquir'd yet who pick'd my pocket?

HOSTESS. Why, Sir John, what do you think, Sir John? Do you think I keep thieves in my house? I have search'd, I have enquired, so has my husband, man by man, boy by boy, servant by servant. The tithe of a hair was never lost in my house before.

FALSTAFF. Ye lie, hostess. Bardolph was shav'd and lost many a hair, and I'll be sworn my pocket was pick'd. Go to, you are a woman, go!

HOSTESS. Who, I? No; I defy thee! God's light, I was never call'd so in mine own house before!

FALSTAFF. Go to, I know you well enough.

HOSTESS. No, Sir John; you do not know me, Sir John. I know you, Sir John. You owe me money, Sir John, and now you pick a quarrel to beguile me of it. I bought you a dozen of shirts to your back.

FALSTAFF. Dowlas, filthy dowlas! I have given them away to bakers' wives; they have made bolters of them.

HOSTESS. Now, as I am a true woman, holland of eight shillings an ell. You owe money here besides, Sir John, for your diet and by-drinkings, and money lent you, four-and-twenty pound.

FALSTAFF. He had his part of it; let him pay.

HOSTESS. He? Alas, he is poor; he hath nothing.

FALSTAFF. How? Poor? Look upon his face. What call you rich? Let them coin his nose, let them coin his cheeks. I'll not pay a denier. What, will you make a younker of me? Shall I not take mine ease in mine inn but I shall have my pocket pick'd? I have lost a seal-ring of my grandfather's worth forty mark.

HOSTESS. O Jesu, I have heard the Prince tell him, I know not how oft, that that ring was copper!

FALSTAFF. How? the Prince is a Jack, a sneak-cup. 'Sblood, an he were here, I would cudgel him like a dog if he would say so.

Enter the PRINCE and POINS, marching; and FALSTAFF meets them, playing upon his truncheon like a fife

How now, lad? Is the wind in that door, i' faith? Must we all march?

BARDOLPH. Yea, two and two, Newgate fashion.

HOSTESS. My lord, I pray you hear me.

PRINCE. What say'st thou, Mistress Quickly? How doth thy husband?
I love him well; he is an honest man.

HOSTESS. Good my lord, hear me.

FALSTAFF. Prithee let her alone and list to me.

PRINCE. What say'st thou, Jack?

FALSTAFF. The other night I fell asleep here behind the arras and had my pocket pick'd. This house is turn'd bawdy house; they pick pockets.

Prince. What didst thou lose, Jack?

FALSTAFF. Wilt thou believe me, Hal? Three or four bonds of forty pound apiece and a seal-ring of my grandfather's.

PRINCE. A trifle, some eightpenny matter.

HOSTESS. So I told him, my lord, and I said I heard

your Grace say so; and, my lord, he speaks most vilely of you, like a foul-mouth'd man as he is, and said he would cudgel you.

PRINCE. What! he did not?

HOSTESS. There's neither faith, truth, nor womanhood in me else.

FALSTAFF. There's no more faith in thee than in a stewed prune, nor no more truth in thee than in a drawn fox; and for woman-hood, Maid Marian may be the deputy's wife of the ward to thee. Go, you thing, go!

HOSTESS. Say, what thing? what thing?

FALSTAFF. What thing? Why, a thing to thank God on.

HOSTESS. I am no thing to thank God on, I would thou shouldst know it! I am an honest man's wife, and, setting thy knight-hood aside, thou art a knave to call me so.

FALSTAFF. Setting thy womanhood aside, thou art a beast to say otherwise.

HOSTESS. Say, what beast, thou knave, thou?

FALSTAFF. What beast? Why, an otter.

PRINCE. An otter, Sir John? Why an otter?

FALSTAFF. Why, she's neither fish nor flesh; a man knows not where to have her.

HOSTESS. Thou art an unjust man in saying so. Thou or any man knows where to have me, thou knave, thou!

PRINCE. Thou say'st true, hostess, and he slanders thee most grossly.

HOSTESS. So he doth you, my lord, and said this other day you ought him a thousand pound.

PRINCE. Sirrah, do I owe you a thousand pound?

FALSTAFF. A thousand pound, Hal? A million! Thy love

is worth a million; thou owest me thy love.

HOSTESS. Nay, my lord, he call'd you Jack and said he would cudgel you.

FALSTAFF. Did I, Bardolph?

BARDOLPH. Indeed, Sir John, you said so.

FALSTAFF. Yea. if he said my ring was copper.

PRINCE. I say, 'tis copper. Darest thou be as good as thy word now?

FALSTAFF. Why, Hal, thou knowest, as thou art but man, I dare; but as thou art Prince, I fear thee as I fear the roaring of the lion's whelp.

PRINCE. And why not as the lion?

FALSTAFF. The King himself is to be feared as the lion. Dost thou think I'll fear thee as I fear thy father? Nay, an I do, I pray God my girdle break.

PRINCE. O, if it should, how would thy guts fall about thy knees! But, sirrah, there's no room for faith, truth, nor honesty in this bosom of thine. It is all fill'd up with guts and midriff. Charge an honest woman with picking thy pocket? Why, thou whoreson, impudent, emboss'd rascal, if there were anything in thy pocket but tavern reckonings, memorandums of bawdy houses, and one poor pennyworth of sugar candy to make thee long-winded- if thy pocket were enrich'd with any other injuries but these, I am a villain. And yet you will stand to it; you will not pocket up wrong. Art thou not ashamed?

FALSTAFF. Dost thou hear, Hal? Thou knowest in the state of innocency Adam fell; and what should poor Jack Falstaff do in the days of villany? Thou seest I have more flesh than another man, and therefore more frailty. You confess then, you pick'd my pocket?

PRINCE. It appears so by the story.

FALSTAFF. Hostess, I forgive thee. Go make ready breakfast. Love thy husband, look to thy servants, cherish thy guests. Thou shalt find me tractable to any honest reason. Thou seest I am pacified. -Still?- Nay, prithee be gone. *[Exit Hostess]* Now, Hal, to the news at court. For the robbery, lad- how is that answered?

PRINCE. O my sweet beef, I must still be good angel to thee. The money is paid back again.

FALSTAFF. O, I do not like that paying back! 'Tis a double labour.

PRINCE. I am good friends with my father, and may do anything.

FALSTAFF. Rob me the exchequer the first thing thou doest, and do it with unwash'd hands too.

BARDOLPH. Do, my lord.

PRINCE. I have procured thee, Jack, a charge of foot.

FALSTAFF. I would it had been of horse. Where shall I find one that can steal well? O for a fine thief of the age of two-and-twenty or thereabouts! I am heinously unprovided. Well, God be thanked for these rebels. They offend none but the virtuous. I laud them, I praise them.

PRINCE. Bardolph!

BARDOLPH. My lord?

PRINCE. Go bear this letter to Lord John of Lancaster, To my brother John; this to my Lord of Westmoreland.
[Exit BARDOLPH]

Go, Poins, to horse, to horse; for thou and I Have thirty miles to ride yet ere dinner time. *[Exit POINS.]* Jack, meet me to-morrow in the Temple Hall At two o'clock in the afternoon.

There shalt thou know thy charge. and there receive Money and order for their furniture.

The land is burning; Percy stands on high;
And either they or we must lower lie.   *Exit*

FALSTAFF. Rare words! brave world! Hostess, my
breakfast, come.
O, I could wish this tavern were my drum!   *Exit*

ACT IV

SCENE I

The rebel camp near Shrewsbury

Enter HARRY HOTSPUR, WORCESTER, and DOUGLAS

HOTSPUR. Well said, my noble Scot. If speaking truth
In this fine age were not thought flattery,
Such attribution should the Douglas have
As not a soldier of this season's stamp
Should go so general current through the world.
By God, I cannot flatter, I defy
The tongues of soothers! but a braver place
In my heart's love hath no man than yourself.
Nay, task me to my word; approve me, lord.

DOUGLAS. Thou art the king of honour.
No man so potent breathes upon the ground
But I will beard him.

Enter one MESSENGER with letters

HOTSPUR. Do so, and 'tis well.-
What letters hast thou there?- I can but thank you.

MESSENGER. These letters come from your father.

HOTSPUR. Letters from him? Why comes he not himself?

MESSENGER. He cannot come, my lord; he is grievous
sick.

HOTSPUR. Zounds! how has he the leisure to be sick
In such a justling time? Who leads his power?
Under whose government come they along?

MESSENGER. His letters bears his mind, not I, my lord.

WORCESTER. I prithee tell me, doth he keep his bed?

MESSENGER. He did, my lord, four days ere I set forth,
And at the time of my departure thence
He was much fear'd by his physicians.

WORCESTER. I would the state of time had first been whole
Ere he by sickness had been visited.
His health was never better worth than now.

HOTSPUR. Sick now? droop now? This sickness doth infect
The very lifeblood of our enterprise.
'Tis catching hither, even to our camp.
He writes me here that inward sickness-
And that his friends by deputation could not
So soon be drawn; no did he think it meet
To lay so dangerous and dear a trust
On any soul remov'd but on his own.
Yet doth he give us bold advertisement,
That with our small conjunction we should on,
To see how fortune is dispos'd to us;
For, as he writes, there is no quailing now,
Because the King is certainly possess'd
Of all our purposes. What say you to it?

WORCESTER. Your father's sickness is a maim to us.

HOTSPUR. A perilous gash, a very limb lopp'd off.
And yet, in faith, it is not! His present want
Seems more than we shall find it. Were it good
To set the exact wealth of all our states
All at one cast? to set so rich a man
On the nice hazard of one doubtful hour?
It were not good; for therein should we read
The very bottom and the soul of hope,
The very list, the very utmost bound
Of all our fortunes.

William Shakespeare

DOUGLAS. Faith, and so we should;
Where now remains a sweet reversion.
We may boldly spend upon the hope of what
Is to come in.
A comfort of retirement lives in this.

HOTSPUR. A rendezvous, a home to fly unto,
If that the devil and mischance look big
Upon the maidenhead of our affairs.

WORCESTER. But yet I would your father had been
here.
The quality and hair of our attempt
Brooks no division. It will be thought
By some that know not why he is away,
That wisdom, loyalty, and mere dislike
Of our proceedings kept the Earl from hence.
And think how such an apprehension
May turn the tide of fearful faction
And breed a kind of question in our cause.
For well you know we of the off'ring side
Must keep aloof from strict arbitrement,
And stop all sight-holes, every loop from whence
The eye of reason may pry in upon us.
This absence of your father's draws a curtain
That shows the ignorant a kind of fear
Before not dreamt of.

HOTSPUR. You strain too far.
I rather of his absence make this use:
It lends a lustre and more great opinion,
A larger dare to our great enterprise,
Than if the Earl were here; for men must think,
If we, without his help, can make a head
To push against a kingdom, with his help
We shall o'erturn it topsy-turvy down.
Yet all goes well; yet all our joints are whole.

DOUGLAS. As heart can think. There is not such a
word

Spoke of in Scotland as this term of fear.

Enter SIR RICHARD VERNON

HOTSPUR. My cousin Vernon! welcome, by my soul.

VERNON. Pray God my news be worth a welcome,
lord.
The Earl of Westmoreland, seven thousand strong,
Is marching hitherwards; with him Prince John.

HOTSPUR. No harm. What more?

VERNON. And further, I have learn'd
The King himself in person is set forth,
Or hitherwards intended speedily,
With strong and mighty preparation.

HOTSPUR. He shall be welcome too. Where is his son,
The nimble-footed madcap Prince of Wales,
And his comrades, that daff'd the world aside
And bid it pass?

VERNON. All furnish'd, all in arms;
All plum'd like estridges that with the wind
Bated like eagles having lately bath'd;
Glittering in golden coats like images;
As full of spirit as the month of May
And gorgeous as the sun at midsummer;
Wanton as youthful goats, wild as young bulls.
I saw young Harry with his beaver on
His cushes on his thighs, gallantly arm'd,
Rise from the ground like feathered Mercury,
And vaulted with such ease into his seat
As if an angel dropp'd down from the clouds
To turn and wind a fiery Pegasus
And witch the world with noble horsemanship.

HOTSPUR. No more, no more! Worse than the sun in
March,
This praise doth nourish agues. Let them come.

William Shakespeare

They come like sacrifices in their trim,
And to the fire-ey'd maid of smoky war
All hot and bleeding Will we offer them.
The mailed Mars Shall on his altar sit
Up to the ears in blood. I am on fire
To hear this rich reprisal is so nigh,
And yet not ours. Come, let me taste my horse,
Who is to bear me like a thunderbolt
Against the bosom of the Prince of Wales.
Harry to Harry shall, hot horse to horse,
Meet, and ne'er part till one drop down a corse.
O that Glendower were come!

VERNON. There is more news.
I learn'd in Worcester, as I rode along,
He cannot draw his power this fourteen days.

DOUGLAS. That's the worst tidings that I hear of yet.

WORCESTER. Ay, by my faith, that bears a frosty
sound.

HOTSPUR. What may the King's whole battle reach
unto?

VERNON. To thirty thousand.

HOTSPUR. Forty let it be.
My father and Glendower being both away,
The powers of us may serve so great a day.
Come, let us take a muster speedily.
Doomsday is near. Die all, die merrily.

DOUGLAS. Talk not of dying. I am out of fear
Of death or death's hand for this one half-year.   *Exeunt*

SCENE II

A public road near Coventry

Enter FALSTAFF and BARDOLPH

FALSTAFF. Bardolph, get thee before to Coventry; fill me a bottle of sack. Our soldiers shall march through. We'll to Sutton Co'fil' to-night.

BARDOLPH. Will you give me money, Captain?

FALSTAFF. Lay out, lay out.

BARDOLPH. This bottle makes an angel.

FALSTAFF. An if it do, take it for thy labour; an if it make twenty, take them all; I'll answer the coinage. Bid my lieutenant Peto meet me at town's end.

BARDOLPH. I Will, Captain. Farewell.   *Exit*

FALSTAFF. If I be not ashamed of my soldiers, I am a sous'd gurnet. I have misused the King's press damnably. I have got in exchange of a hundred and fifty soldiers, three hundred and odd pounds. I press me none but good householders, yeomen's sons; inquire me out contracted bachelors, such as had been ask'd twice on the banes- such a commodity of warm slaves as had as lieve hear the devil as a drum; such as fear the report of a caliver worse than a struck fowl or a hurt wild duck. I press'd me none but such toasts-and-butter, with hearts in their bellies no bigger than pins' heads, and they have bought out their services; and now my whole charge consists of ancients, corporals, lieutenants, gentlemen of companies- slaves as ragged as Lazarus in the painted cloth, where the glutton's dogs licked his sores; and such as indeed were never soldiers, but discarded unjust serving-men, younger sons to Younger brothers, revolted tapsters, and ostlers trade-fall'n; the cankers of a calm world and a long peace; ten times more dishonourable ragged than an old fac'd ancient; and such have I to fill up the rooms of them that have bought out their services that you would think that I had a hundred and fifty tattered Prodigals lately come from swine-keeping, from eating draff and husks. A mad fellow met me on the way, and told me I had unloaded all the gibbets and press'd the dead bodies. No eye hath seen such scarecrows. I'll not march through Coventry with them, that's flat. Nay, and the villains march wide betwixt the legs, as if they had gyves on; for indeed I had the most of them out of prison. There's but a shirt and a half in all my company; and the half-shirt is two napkins tack'd together and thrown over the shoulders like a herald's coat without sleeves; and the shirt, to say the truth, stol'n from my host at Saint Alban's, or the red-nose innkeeper of Daventry. But that's all one; they'll find linen enough on every hedge.

Enter the PRINCE and the LORD OF WESTMORELAND

PRINCE. How now, blown Jack? How now, quilt?

FALSTAFF. What, Hal? How now, mad wag? What a devil dost thou in Warwickshire? My good Lord of Westmoreland, I cry you mercy. I thought your honour had already been at Shrewsbury.

EARL OF WESTMORELAND. Faith, Sir John, 'tis more than time that I were there, and you too; but my powers are there already. The King, I can tell you, looks for us all. We must away all, to-night.

FALSTAFF. Tut, never fear me. I am as vigilant as a cat to steal cream.

PRINCE. I think, to steal cream indeed, for thy theft hath already made thee butter. But tell me, Jack, whose fellows are these that come after?

FALSTAFF. Mine, Hal, mine.

PRINCE. I did never see such pitiful rascals.

FALSTAFF. Tut, tut! good enough to toss; food for powder, food for powder. They'll fill a pit as well as better. Tush, man, mortal men, mortal men.

EARL OF WESTMORELAND. Ay, but, Sir John, methinks they are exceeding poor and bare- too beggarly.

FALSTAFF. Faith, for their poverty, I know, not where they had that; and for their bareness, I am surd they never learn'd that of me.

PRINCE. No, I'll be sworn, unless you call three fingers on the ribs bare. But, sirrah, make haste. Percy 's already in the field.   *Exit*

FALSTAFF. What, is the King encamp'd?

EARL OF WESTMORELAND. He is, Sir John. I fear we shall stay too long.   *Exit*

FALSTAFF. Well,
To the latter end of a fray and the beginning of a feast
Fits a dull fighter and a keen guest.   *Exit*

SCENE III

The rebel camp near Shrewsbury

Enter HOTSPUR, WORCESTER, DOUGLAS,
VERNON

HOTSPUR. We'll fight with him to-night.

WORCESTER. It may not be.

DOUGLAS. You give him then advantage.

VERNON. Not a whit.

HOTSPUR. Why say you so? Looks he no for supply?

VERNON. So do we.

HOTSPUR. His is certain, ours 's doubtful.

WORCESTER. Good cousin, be advis'd; stir not to-night.

VERNON. Do not, my lord.

DOUGLAS. You do not counsel well.
You speak it out of fear and cold heart.

VERNON. Do me no slander, Douglas. By my life-
And I dare well maintain it with my life-
If well-respected honour bid me on
I hold as little counsel with weak fear
As you, my lord, or any Scot that this day lives.
Let it be seen to-morrow in the battle
Which of us fears.

DOUGLAS. Yea, or to-night.

VERNON. Content.

HOTSPUR. To-night, say I.
Come, come, it may not be. I wonder much,
Being men of such great leading as you are,
That you foresee not what impediments
Drag back our expedition. Certain horse
Of my cousin Vernon's are not yet come up.
Your uncle Worcester's horse came but to-day;
And now their pride and mettle is asleep,
Their courage with hard labour tame and dull,
That not a horse is half the half of himself.

HOTSPUR. So are the horses of the enemy,
In general journey-bated and brought low.
The better part of ours are full of rest.

WORCESTER. The number of the King exceedeth
ours.
For God's sake, cousin, stay till all come in.

The trumpet sounds a parley. Enter SIR WALTER BLUNT

BLUNT. I come with gracious offers from the King,
If you vouchsafe me hearing and respect.

HOTSPUR. Welcome, Sir Walter Blunt, and would to God
You were of our determination!
Some of us love you well; and even those some
Envy your great deservings and good name,
Because you are not of our quality,
But stand against us like an enemy.

BLUNT. And God defend but still I should stand so,
So long as out of limit and true rule
You stand against anointed majesty!
But to my charge. The King hath sent to know
The nature of your griefs; and whereupon
You conjure from the breast of civil peace
Such bold hostility, teaching his duteous land
Audacious cruelty. If that the King
Have any way your good deserts forgot,
Which he confesseth to be manifold,
He bids you name your griefs, and with all speed
You shall have your desires with interest,
And pardon absolute for yourself and these
Herein misled by your suggestion.

HOTSPUR. The King is kind; and well we know the King
Knows at what time to promise, when to pay.
My father and my uncle and myself
Did give him that same royalty he wears;
And when he was not six-and-twenty strong,
Sick in the world's regard, wretched and low,
A poor unminded outlaw sneaking home,
My father gave him welcome to the shore;
And when he heard him swear and vow to God
He came but to be Duke of Lancaster,
To sue his livery and beg his peace,
With tears of innocency and terms of zeal,

My father, in kind heart and pity mov'd,
Swore him assistance, and performed it too.
Now, when the lords and barons of the realm
Perceiv'd Northumberland did lean to him,
The more and less came in with cap and knee;
Met him on boroughs, cities, villages,
Attended him on bridges, stood in lanes,
Laid gifts before him, proffer'd him their oaths,
Give him their heirs as pages, followed him
Even at the heels in golden multitudes.
He presently, as greatness knows itself,
Steps me a little higher than his vow
Made to my father, while his blood was poor,
Upon the naked shore at Ravenspurgh;
And now, forsooth, takes on him to reform
Some certain edicts and some strait decrees
That lie too heavy on the commonwealth;
Cries out upon abuses, seems to weep
Over his country's wrongs; and by this face,
This seeming brow of justice, did he win
The hearts of all that he did angle for;
Proceeded further- cut me off the heads
Of all the favourites that the absent King
In deputation left behind him here
When he was personal in the Irish war.
But. Tut! I came not to hear this.

HOTSPUR. Then to the point.
In short time after lie depos'd the King;
Soon after that depriv'd him of his life;
And in the neck of that task'd the whole state;
To make that worse, suff'red his kinsman March
(Who is, if every owner were well placid,
Indeed his king) to be engag'd in Wales,
There without ransom to lie forfeited;
Disgrac'd me in my happy victories,
Sought to entrap me by intelligence;
Rated mine uncle from the Council board;

In rage dismiss'd my father from the court;
Broke an oath on oath, committed wrong on wrong;
And in conclusion drove us to seek out
This head of safety, and withal to pry
Into his title, the which we find
Too indirect for long continuance.

BLUNT. Shall I return this answer to the King?

HOTSPUR. Not so, Sir Walter. We'll withdraw awhile.
Go to the King; and let there be impawn'd
Some surety for a safe return again,
And In the morning early shall mine uncle
Bring him our purposes; and so farewell.

BLUNT. I would you would accept of grace and love.

HOTSPUR. And may be so we shall.

BLUNT. Pray God you do.   *Exeunt*

SCENE IV

York. The Archbishop's Palace

Enter the ARCHBISHOP OF YORK and SIR MICHAEL

ARCHBISHOP OF YORK. Hie, good Sir Michael;
bear this sealed brief
With winged haste to the Lord Marshal;
This to my cousin Scroop; and all the rest
To whom they are directed. If you knew
How much they do import, you would make haste.
Sir M. My good lord,
I guess their tenour.
Arch. Like enough you do.
To-morrow, good Sir Michael, is a day
Wherein the fortune of ten thousand men
Must bide the touch; for, sir, at Shrewsbury,
As I am truly given to understand,

The King with mighty and quick-raised power
Meets with Lord Harry; and I fear, Sir Michael,
What with the sickness of Northumberland,
Whose power was in the first proportion,
And what with Owen Glendower's absence thence,
Who with them was a rated sinew too
And comes not in, overrul'd by prophecies-
I fear the power of Percy is too weak
To wage an instant trial with the King.

SIR MICHAEL. Why, my good lord, you need not fear;
There is Douglas and Lord Mortimer.

ARCHBISHOP OF YORK. No, Mortimer is not there.

SIR MICHAEL. But there is Mordake, Vernon, Lord
Harry Percy,
And there is my Lord of Worcester, and a head
Of gallant warriors, noble gentlemen.

ARCHBISHOP OF YORK. And so there is; but yet the
King hath drawn
The special head of all the land together-
The Prince of Wales, Lord John of Lancaster,
The noble Westmoreland and warlike Blunt,
And many moe corrivals and dear men
Of estimation and command in arms.

SIR MICHAEL. Doubt not, my lord, they shall be well
oppos'd.

ARCHBISHOP OF YORK. I hope no less, yet needful
'tis to fear;
And, to prevent the worst, Sir Michael, speed.
For if Lord Percy thrive not, ere the King
Dismiss his power, he means to visit us,
For he hath heard of our confederacy,
And 'tis but wisdom to make strong against him.
Therefore make haste. I must go write again
To other friends; and so farewell, Sir Michael.   *Exeunt*

ACT V

SCENE I

The King's camp near Shrewsbury

*Enter the KING, PRINCE OF WALES, LORD JOHN
OF LANCASTER, SIR WALTER BLUNT, FALSTAFF*

KING. How bloodily the sun begins to peer
Above yon busky hill! The day looks pale
At his distemp'rature.

PRINCE. The southern wind
Doth play the trumpet to his purposes
And by his hollow whistling in the leaves
Foretells a tempest and a blust'ring day.

KING. Theft with the losers let it sympathize,
For nothing can seem foul to those that win.

The trumpet sounds. Enter WORCESTER and VERNON

How, now, my Lord of Worcester? 'Tis not well
That you and I should meet upon such terms
As now we meet. You have deceiv'd our trust
And made us doff our easy robes of peace
To crush our old limbs in ungentle steel.
This is not well, my lord; this is not well.
What say you to it? Will you again unknit
This churlish knot of all-abhorred war,
And move in that obedient orb again
Where you did give a fair and natural light,
And be no more an exhal'd meteor,
A prodigy of fear, and a portent
Of broached mischief to the unborn times?

WORCESTER. Hear me, my liege.
For mine own part, I could be well content
To entertain the lag-end of my life

William Shakespeare

With quiet hours; for I do protest
I have not sought the day of this dislike.

KING. You have not sought it! How comes it then,

FALSTAFF. Rebellion lay in his way, and he found it.

PRINCE. Peace, chewet, peace!

WORCESTER. It pleas'd your Majesty to turn your
looks
Of favour from myself and all our house;
And yet I must remember you, my lord,
We were the first and dearest of your friends.
For you my staff of office did I break
In Richard's time, and posted day and night
To meet you on the way and kiss your hand
When yet you were in place and in account
Nothing so strong and fortunate as I.
It was myself, my brother, and his son
That brought you home and boldly did outdare
The dangers of the time. You swore to us,
And you did swear that oath at Doncaster,
That you did nothing purpose 'gainst the state,
Nor claim no further than your new-fall'n right,
The seat of Gaunt, dukedom of Lancaster.
To this we swore our aid. But in short space
It it rain'd down fortune show'ring on your head,
And such a flood of greatness fell on you-
What with our help, what with the absent King,
What with the injuries of a wanton time,
The seeming sufferances that you had borne,
And the contrarious winds that held the King
So long in his unlucky Irish wars
That all in England did repute him dead-
And from this swarm of fair advantages
You took occasion to be quickly woo'd
To gripe the general sway into your hand;
Forgot your oath to us at Doncaster;
And, being fed by us, you us'd us so

As that ungentle gull, the cuckoo's bird,
Useth the sparrow- did oppress our nest;
Grew, by our feeding to so great a bulk
That even our love thirst not come near your sight
For fear of swallowing; but with nimble wing
We were enforc'd for safety sake to fly
Out of your sight and raise this present head;
Whereby we stand opposed by such means
As you yourself have forg'd against yourself
By unkind usage, dangerous countenance,
And violation of all faith and troth
Sworn to tis in your younger enterprise.

KING. These things, indeed, you have articulate,
Proclaim'd at market crosses, read in churches,
To face the garment of rebellion
With some fine colour that may please the eye
Of fickle changelings and poor discontents,
Which gape and rub the elbow at the news
Of hurlyburly innovation.
And never yet did insurrection want
Such water colours to impaint his cause,
Nor moody beggars, starving for a time
Of pell-mell havoc and confusion.

PRINCE. In both our armies there is many a soul
Shall pay full dearly for this encounter,
If once they join in trial. Tell your nephew
The Prince of Wales doth join with all the world
In praise of Henry Percy. By my hopes,
This present enterprise set off his head,
I do not think a braver gentleman,
More active-valiant or more valiant-young,
More daring or more bold, is now alive
To grace this latter age with noble deeds.
For my part, I may speak it to my shame,
I have a truant been to chivalry;
And so I hear he doth account me too.
Yet this before my father's Majesty-

I am content that he shall take the odds
Of his great name and estimation,
And will to save the blood on either side,
Try fortune with him in a single fight.

KING. And, Prince of Wales, so dare we venture thee,
Albeit considerations infinite
Do make against it. No, good Worcester, no!
We love our people well; even those we love
That are misled upon your cousin's part;
And, will they take the offer of our grace,
Both he, and they, and you, yea, every man
Shall be my friend again, and I'll be his.
So tell your cousin, and bring me word
What he will do. But if he will not yield,
Rebuke and dread correction wait on us,
And they shall do their office. So be gone.
We will not now be troubled with reply.
We offer fair; take it advisedly.

Exit WORCESTER with VERNON

PRINCE. It will not be accepted, on my life.
The Douglas and the Hotspur both together
Are confident against the world in arms.

KING. Hence, therefore, every leader to his charge;
For, on their answer, will we set on them,
And God befriend us as our cause is just!

Exeunt all but PRINCE and FALSTAFF

FALSTAFF. Hal, if thou see me down in the battle and
bestride me, so!
'Tis a point of friendship.

PRINCE. Nothing but a Colossus can do thee that
friendship.
Say thy prayers, and farewell.

FALSTAFF. I would 'twere bedtime, Hal, and all well.

PRINCE. Why, thou owest God a death.   *Exit*

FALSTAFF. 'Tis not due yet. I would be loath to pay him before his day. What need I be so forward with him that calls not on me? Well, 'tis no matter; honour pricks me on. Yea, but how if honour prick me off when I come on? How then? Can honor set to a leg? No. Or an arm? No. Or take away the grief of a wound? No. Honour hath no skill in surgery then? No. What is honour? A word. What is that word honour? Air. A trim reckoning! Who hath it? He that died a Wednesday. Doth he feel it? No. Doth be bear it? No. 'Tis insensible then? Yea, to the dead. But will it not live with the living? No. Why? Detraction will not suffer it. Therefore I'll none of it. Honour is a mere scutcheon- and so ends my catechism.   *Exit*

SCENE II

The rebel camp

Enter WORCESTER and SIR RICHARD VERNON

WORCESTER. O no, my nephew must not know, Sir Richard,
The liberal and kind offer of the King.

VERNON. 'Twere best he did.

WORCESTER. Then are we all undone.
It is not possible, it cannot be
The King should keep his word in loving us.
He will suspect us still and find a time
To punish this offence in other faults.
Suspicion all our lives shall be stuck full of eyes;
For treason is but trusted like the fox
Who, ne'er so tame, so cherish'd and lock'd up,
Will have a wild trick of his ancestors.
Look how we can, or sad or merrily,
Interpretation will misquote our looks,
And we shall feed like oxen at a stall,

The better cherish'd, still the nearer death.
My nephew's trespass may be well forgot;
It hath the excuse of youth and heat of blood,
And an adopted name of privilege-
A hare-brained Hotspur govern'd by a spleen.
All his offences live upon my head
And on his father's. We did train him on;
And, his corruption being taken from us,
We, as the spring of all, shall pay for all.
Therefore, good cousin, let not Harry know,
In any case, the offer of the King.

Enter HOTSPUR and DOUGLAS

VERNON. Deliver what you will, I'll say 'tis so.
Here comes your cousin.

HOTSPUR. My uncle is return'd.
Deliver up my Lord of Westmoreland.
Uncle, what news?

WORCESTER. The King will bid you battle presently.

DOUGLAS. Defy him by the Lord Of Westmoreland.

HOTSPUR. Lord Douglas, go you and tell him so.

DOUGLAS. Marry, and shall, and very willingly. *Exit*

WORCESTER. There is no seeming mercy in the King.

HOTSPUR. Did you beg any, God forbid!

WORCESTER. I told him gently of our grievances,
Of his oath-breaking; which he mended thus,
By now forswearing that he is forsworn.
He calls us rebels, traitors, aid will scourge
With haughty arms this hateful name in us.

Enter DOUGLAS

DOUGLAS. Arm, gentlemen! to arms! for I

have thrown
A brave defiance in King Henry's teeth,
And Westmoreland, that was engag'd, did bear it;
Which cannot choose but bring him quickly on.

WORCESTER. The Prince of Wales stepp'd forth
before the King
And, nephew, challeng'd you to single fight.

HOTSPUR. O, would the quarrel lay upon our heads,
And that no man might draw short breath to-day
But I and Harry Monmouth! Tell me, tell me,
How show'd his tasking? Seem'd it in contempt?
No, by my soul. I never in my life
Did hear a challenge urg'd more modestly,
Unless a brother should a brother dare
To gentle exercise and proof of arms.
He gave you all the duties of a man;
Trimm'd up your praises with a princely tongue;
Spoke your deservings like a chronicle;
Making you ever better than his praise
By still dispraising praise valued with you;
And, which became him like a prince indeed,
He made a blushing cital of himself,
And chid his truant youth with such a grace
As if lie mast'red there a double spirit
Of teaching and of learning instantly.
There did he pause; but let me tell the world,
If he outlive the envy of this day,
England did never owe so sweet a hope,
So much misconstrued in his wantonness.

HOTSPUR. Cousin, I think thou art enamoured
Upon his follies. Never did I hear
Of any prince so wild a libertine.
But be he as he will, yet once ere night
I will embrace him with a soldier's arm,
That he shall shrink under my courtesy.
Arm, arm with speed! and, fellows, soldiers, friends,

Better consider what you have to do
Than I, that have not well the gift of tongue,
Can lift your blood up with persuasion.

Enter a MESSENGER

MESSENGER. My lord, here are letters for you.

HOTSPUR. I cannot read them now.-
O gentlemen, the time of life is short!
To spend that shortness basely were too long
If life did ride upon a dial's point,
Still ending at the arrival of an hour.
An if we live, we live to tread on kings;
If die, brave death, when princes die with us!
Now for our consciences, the arms are fair,
When the intent of bearing them is just.

Enter another MESSENGER

MESSENGER. My lord, prepare. The King comes on
apace.

HOTSPUR. I thank him that he cuts me from my tale,
For I profess not talking. Only this-
Let each man do his best; and here draw I
A sword whose temper I intend to stain
With the best blood that I can meet withal
In the adventure of this perilous day.
Now, Esperance! Percy! and set on.
Sound all the lofty instruments of war,
And by that music let us all embrace;
For, heaven to earth, some of us never shall
A second time do such a courtesy. *[Here they embrace.*
The trumpets sound]   *Exeunt*

SCENE III

Plain between the camps

The KING enters with his Power. Alarum to the battle.
Then enter DOUGLAS and SIR WALTER BLUNT

BLUNT. What is thy name, that in the battle thus
Thou crossest me? What honour dost thou seek
Upon my head?

DOUGLAS. Know then my name is Douglas,
And I do haunt thee in the battle thus
Because some tell me that thou art a king.

BLUNT. They tell thee true.

DOUGLAS. The Lord of Stafford dear to-day hath
bought
Thy likeness; for instead of thee, King Harry,
This sword hath ended him. So shall it thee,
Unless thou yield thee as my prisoner.

BLUNT. I was not born a yielder, thou proud Scot;
And thou shalt find a king that will revenge
Lord Stafford's death.

They fight. DOUGLAS kills BLUNT. Then enter
HOTSPUR

HOTSPUR. O Douglas, hadst thou fought at
Holmedon thus,
I never had triumph'd upon a Scot.

DOUGLAS. All's done, all's won. Here breathless lies the
King.

HOTSPUR. Where?

DOUGLAS. Here.

HOTSPUR. This, Douglas? No. I know this face

William Shakespeare

full well.
A gallant knight he was, his name was Blunt;
Semblably furnish'd like the King himself.

DOUGLAS. A fool go with thy soul, whither it goes!
A borrowed title hast thou bought too dear:
Why didst thou tell me that thou wert a king?

HOTSPUR. The King hath many marching in his coats.

DOUGLAS. Now, by my sword, I will kill all his coats;
I'll murder all his wardrop, piece by piece,
Until I meet the King.

HOTSPUR. Up and away!
Our soldiers stand full fairly for the day.   *Exeunt*

Alarum. Enter FALSTAFF solus

FALSTAFF. Though I could scape shot-free at London, I
fear the shot here. Here's no scoring but upon the pate.
Soft! who are you? Sir Walter Blunt. There's honour for
you! Here's no vanity! I am as hot as molten lead, and as
heavy too. God keep lead out of me! I need no more
weight than mine own bowels. I have led my rag-of-
muffins where they are pepper'd. There's not three of my
hundred and fifty left alive; and they are for the town's
end, to beg during life. But who comes here?

Enter the PRINCE

PRINCE. What, stand'st thou idle here? Lend me thy
sword.
Many a nobleman lies stark and stiff
Under the hoofs of vaunting enemies,
Whose deaths are yet unreveng'd. I prithee
Rend me thy sword.

FALSTAFF. O Hal, I prithee give me leave to breathe
awhile. Turk Gregory never did such deeds in arms as I
have done this day. I have paid Percy; I have made

him sure.

PRINCE. He is indeed, and living to kill thee. I prithee lend me thy sword.

FALSTAFF. Nay, before God, Hal, if Percy be alive, thou get'st not my sword; but take my pistol, if thou wilt.

PRINCE. Give it me. What, is it in the case?

FALSTAFF. Ay, Hal. 'Tis hot, 'tis hot. There's that will sack a city. *[The Prince draws it out and finds it to be a bottle of sack.]*

What, is it a time to jest and dally now? *[He throws the bottle at him]* *Exit*

FALSTAFF. Well, if Percy be alive, I'll pierce him. If he do come in my way, so; if he do not, if I come in his willingly, let him make a carbonado of me. I like not such grinning honour as Sir Walter hath. Give me life; which if I can save, so; if not, honour comes unlook'd for, and there's an end. *Exit*

SCENE IV

Another part of the field

Alarum. Excursions. Enter the KING, the PRINCE, LORD JOHN OF LANCASTER, EARL OF WESTMORELAND

KING. I prithee,
Harry, withdraw thyself; thou bleedest too much.
Lord John of Lancaster, go you unto him.
John. Not I, my lord, unless I did bleed too.

PRINCE. I do beseech your Majesty make up,
Lest Your retirement do amaze your friends.

KING. I will do so.

My Lord of Westmoreland, lead him to his tent.

EARL OF WESTMORELAND. Come, my lord, I'll lead you to your tent.

PRINCE. Lead me, my lord, I do not need your help;
And God forbid a shallow scratch should drive
The Prince of Wales from such a field as this,
Where stain'd nobility lies trodden on,
And rebels' arms triumph in massacres!

JOHN. We breathe too long. Come, cousin Westmoreland,
Our duty this way lies. For God's sake, come.
        Exeunt PRINCE JOHN and WESTMORELAND

PRINCE. By God, thou hast deceiv'd me, Lancaster!
I did not think thee lord of such a spirit.
Before, I lov'd thee as a brother, John;
But now, I do respect thee as my soul.

KING. I saw him hold Lord Percy at the point
With lustier maintenance than I did look for
Of such an ungrown warrior.

PRINCE. O, this boy
Lends mettle to us all!   *Exit*

                Enter DOUGLAS

DOUGLAS. Another king? They grow like Hydra's heads.
I am the Douglas, fatal to all those
That wear those colours on them. What art thou
That counterfeit'st the person of a king?

KING. The King himself, who, Douglas, grieves at heart
So many of his shadows thou hast met,
And not the very King. I have two boys
Seek Percy and thyself about the field;
But, seeing thou fall'st on me so luckily,

I will assay thee. So defend thyself.

DOUGLAS. I fear thou art another counterfeit;
And yet, in faith, thou bearest thee like a king.
But mine I am sure thou art, whoe'er thou be,
And thus I win thee.

They fight. The King being in danger, enter PRINCE OF WALES

PRINCE. Hold up thy head, vile Scot, or thou art like
Never to hold it up again! The spirits
Of valiant Shirley, Stafford, Blunt are in my arms.
It is the Prince of Wales that threatens thee,
Who never promiseth but he means to pay. *[They fight. Douglas flieth]*
Cheerly, my lord. How fares your Grace?
Sir Nicholas Gawsey hath for succour sent,
And so hath Clifton. I'll to Clifton straight.

KING. Stay and breathe awhile.
Thou hast redeem'd thy lost opinion,
And show'd thou mak'st some tender of my life,
In this fair rescue thou hast brought to me.

PRINCE. O God! they did me too much injury
That ever said I heark'ned for your death.
If it were so, I might have let alone
The insulting hand of Douglas over you,
Which would have been as speedy in your end
As all the poisonous potions in the world,
And sav'd the treacherous labour of your son.

KING. Make up to Clifton; I'll to Sir Nicholas Gawsey.

Exit

Enter HOTSPUR

HOTSPUR. If I mistake not, thou art Harry Monmouth.

PRINCE. Thou speak'st as if I would deny my name.

HOTSPUR. My name is Harry Percy.

PRINCE. Why, then I see
A very valiant rebel of the name.
I am the Prince of Wales; and think not, Percy,
To share with me in glory any more.
Two stars keep not their motion in one sphere,
Nor can one England brook a double reign
Of Harry Percy and the Prince of Wales.

HOTSPUR. Nor shall it, Harry; for the hour is come
To end the one of us and would to God
Thy name in arms were now as great as mine!

PRINCE. I'll make it greater ere I part from thee,
And all the budding honours on thy crest
I'll crop to make a garland for my head.

HOTSPUR. I can no longer brook thy vanities.
[They fight]

Enter FALSTAFF

FALSTAFF. Well said, Hal! to it, Hal! Nay, you shall find
no boy's play here, I can tell you.

Enter DOUGLAS

*[He fighteth with Falstaff, who falls down as if he were
dead. [Exit Douglas] The Prince killeth Percy]*

HOTSPUR. O Harry, thou hast robb'd me of my
youth!
I better brook the loss of brittle life
Than those proud titles thou hast won of me.
They wound my thoughts worse than thy sword my
flesh.
But thoughts the slave, of life, and life time's fool,
And time, that takes survey of all the world,
Must have a stop. O, I could prophesy,
But that the earthy and cold hand of death

Lies on my tongue. No, Percy, thou art dust,
And food for- *[Dies]*

PRINCE. For worms, brave Percy. Fare thee well, great
heart!
Ill-weav'd ambition, how much art thou shrunk!
When that this body did contain a spirit,
A kingdom for it was too small a bound;
But now two paces of the vilest earth
Is room enough. This earth that bears thee dead
Bears not alive so stout a gentleman.
If thou wert sensible of courtesy,
I should not make so dear a show of zeal.
But let my favours hide thy mangled face;
And, even in thy behalf, I'll thank myself
For doing these fair rites of tenderness.
Adieu, and take thy praise with thee to heaven!
Thy ignominy sleep with thee in the grave,
But not rememb'red in thy epitaph!
He spieth Falstaff on the ground.
What, old acquaintance? Could not all this flesh
Keep in a little life? Poor Jack, farewell!
I could have better spar'd a better man.
O, I should have a heavy miss of thee
If I were much in love with vanity!
Death hath not struck so fat a deer to-day,
Though many dearer, in this bloody fray.
Embowell'd will I see thee by-and-by;
Till then in blood by noble Percy lie.   *Exit*

[Falstaff riseth up]

FALSTAFF. Embowell'd? If thou embowel me to-day, I'll
give you leave to powder me and eat me too to-morrow.
'Sblood, 'twas time to counterfeit, or that hot termagant
Scot had paid me scot and lot too. Counterfeit? I lie; I am
no counterfeit. To die is to be a counterfeit; for he is but
the counterfeit of a man who hath not the life of a man;
but to counterfeit dying when a man thereby liveth, is to

be no counterfeit, but the true and perfect image of life indeed. The better part of valour is discretion; in the which better part I have saved my life. Zounds, I am afraid of this gunpowder Percy, though he be dead. How if he should counterfeit too, and rise? By my faith, I am afraid he would prove the better counterfeit. Therefore I'll make him sure; yea, and I'll swear I kill'd him. Why may not he rise as well as I? Nothing confutes me but eyes, and nobody sees me. Therefore, sirrah *[Stabs him]*, with a new wound in your thigh, come you along with me. *[He takes up Hotspur on his back]*

Enter PRINCE, and JOHN OF LANCASTER

PRINCE. Come, brother John; full bravely hast thou flesh'd
Thy maiden sword.

JOHN. But, soft! whom have we here?
Did you not tell me this fat man was dead?

PRINCE. I did; I saw him dead,
Breathless and bleeding on the ground. Art thou alive,
Or is it fantasy that plays upon our eyesight?
I prithee speak. We will not trust our eyes
Without our ears. Thou art not what thou seem'st.

FALSTAFF. No, that's certain! I am not a double man; but if I be not Jack Falstaff, then am I a Jack. There 's Percy. If your father will do me any honour, so; if not, let him kill the next Percy himself. I look to be either earl or duke, I can assure you.

PRINCE. Why, Percy I kill'd myself, and saw thee dead!

FALSTAFF. Didst thou? Lord, Lord, how this world is given to lying! I grant you I was down, and out of breath, and so was he; but we rose both at an instant and fought a long hour by Shrewsbury clock. If I may be believ'd, so; if not, let them that should reward valour bear the sin upon their own heads. I'll take it upon my death, I gave

him this wound in the thigh. If the man were alive and
would deny it, zounds! I would make him eat a piece of
my sword.

JOHN. This is the strangest tale that ever I beard.

PRINCE. This is the strangest fellow, brother John.
Come, bring your luggage nobly on your back.
For my part, if a lie may do thee grace,
I'll gild it with the happiest terms I have.
[A retreat is sounded]

The trumpet sounds retreat; the day is ours.
Come, brother, let's to the highest of the field,
To see what friends are living, who are dead.
         Exeunt PRINCE HENRY and PRINCE JOHN

FALSTAFF. I'll follow, as they say, for reward. He that
rewards me, God reward him! If I do grow great, I'll
grow less; for I'll purge, and leave sack, and live cleanly,
as a nobleman should do.   *Exit bearing off the body*

SCENE V

Another part of the field

*The trumpets sound. Enter the KING, PRINCE OF
WALES, LORD JOHN OF LANCASTER,EARL OF
WESTMORELAND, with WORCESTER and VERNON
prisoners*

KING. Thus ever did rebellion find rebuke.
Ill-spirited Worcester! did not we send grace,
Pardon, and terms of love to all of you?
And wouldst thou turn our offers contrary?
Misuse the tenour of thy kinsman's trust?
Three knights upon our party slain to-day,
A noble earl, and many a creature else
Had been alive this hour,

If like a Christian thou hadst truly borne
Betwixt our armies true intelligence.

WORCESTER. What I have done my safety urg'd me
to;
And I embrace this fortune patiently,
Since not to be avoided it fails on me.

KING. Bear Worcester to the death, and Vernon too;
Other offenders we will pause upon.
        Exeunt WORCESTER and VERNON, guarded

How goes the field?

PRINCE. The noble Scot, Lord Douglas, when he saw
The fortune of the day quite turn'd from him,
The Noble Percy slain and all his men
Upon the foot of fear, fled with the rest;
And falling from a hill,he was so bruis'd
That the pursuers took him. At my tent
The Douglas is, and I beseech Your Grace
I may dispose of him.

KING. With all my heart.

PRINCE. Then brother John of Lancaster, to you
This honourable bounty shall belong.
Go to the Douglas and deliver him
Up to his pleasure, ransomless and free.
His valour shown upon our crests today
Hath taught us how to cherish such high deeds,
Even in the bosom of our adversaries.

JOHN. I thank your Grace for this high courtesy,
Which I shall give away immediately.

KING. Then this remains, that we divide our power.
You, son John, and my cousin Westmoreland,
Towards York shall bend you with your dearest speed
To meet Northumberland and the prelate Scroop,
Who, as we hear, are busily in arms.
Myself and you, son Harry, will towards Wales

To fight with Glendower and the Earl of March.
Rebellion in this laud shall lose his sway,
Meeting the check of such another day;
And since this business so fair is done,
Let us not leave till all our own be won.   *Exeunt*

THE END

LaVergne, TN USA
30 March 2011
222148LV00002B/3/A

9 781421 813462